W9-AOY-724

Main Currents
in
Early Christian Thought

BOARD OF EDITORS

John E. Lynch, C.S.P. (General Editor)
Professor of Church History
St. Paul's College

Thomas P. Collins
Instructor in Theology
Manhattan College

Johannes Quasten
Professor of Ancient Church History
and Christian Archaeology
Catholic University of America

Wilfred F. Dewan, C.S.P.
Professor of Dogmatic Theology
St. Paul's College

Thomas F. Finn, C.S.P.
Professor of Sacramental Theology
St. Paul's College

Walter J. Burghardt, S.J.
Professor of Patrology and Archaeology
Woodstock College

Eugene M. Burke, C.S.P.
Professor of Dogmatic Theology
Catholic University of America

Gerard S. Sloyan
Professor of Religious Education
Catholic University of America

ST. JOSEPH'S UNIVERSITY

3 9353 00225 3233

Main Currents
in
Early Christian Thought

by

ROBERT BARR, S.J.

Preface by
Jean Daniélou

BT9
31
B26

BT
25
B2K

111497

PAULIST PRESS   GLEN ROCK, N.J.

IMPRIMI POTEST: Very Rev. Linus J. Thro, S.J.
                   Provincial, Missouri Province

August 24, 1965

NIHIL OBSTAT: Robert E. Hunt, S.T.D.
                 Censor Librorum

IMPRIMATUR: ✠ Thomas A. Boland, S.T.D.
              Archbishop of Newark

July 21, 1966

Copyright © 1966 by
The Missionary Society
of St. Paul the Apostle
in the State of New York

Library of Congress
Catalog Card Number: 66-22055

Cover Design: Claude Ponsot

Published by Paulist Press
Editorial Office: 304 W. 58th St., N.Y., N.Y. 10019
Business Office: Glen Rock, New Jersey 07452

Printed and bound in the
United States of America

CONTENTS

PREFACE

One of the finest things about contemporary religious thought is the renewal of patristic theology, a renewal prepared by the scientific efforts that have permitted the restoration of this theology to its historical, cultural and linguistic context. But patristic theology should not merely be an object of erudition. It is one of the sources of contemporary theological research. It is not only of interest to specialists, but it is also especially important for all Christians who desire to give expression to their faith.

In this regard, Father Robert Barr's book is of great interest. Basing himself on a solid knowledge of patrology, he seeks to indicate the great themes of thought in the fathers of the Church. In this sense his book furnishes a very sure guide for one who wishes to orient himself in the vast realm of patrology. More than that, he indicates the main problems the fathers faced and how these were resolved. He simultaneously enables the reader to find what the fathers of the Church are able to give us that is essential, and what belongs to a specific method of thought.

Father Barr's book will interest all those for whom the world of the fathers is a realm fascinating and mysterious. It stimulates the desire for direct contact with the texts themselves. It also constitutes an important contribution to patristic studies. As one consequence of this the book makes an important contribution to theological research of the post-conciliar period.

JEAN DANIÉLOU

FOREWORD

Theology is historical: Without being identified with history, it has its origins in place and time, in cultures and civilization, in temperaments and mentalities. Theology is human thought, and currents of thought have their history. Yet "currents of thought" are not concrete realities; in a sense there are no currents of thought; there are only thinkers. This is our reason for presenting a survey of the currents of patristic thought in a chronological résumé of the main concerns of patristic thinkers.

The present booklet is the first in a series whose subsequent volumes are devoted to patristic readings and commentary, arranged according to subject matter. Since the succeeding volumes will emphasize the texts of the fathers, keeping their history in a secondary role, it seemed important at the start to give the student an opportunity to orient himself historically. This book, then, which presents the currents of theological thought as incarnate in its thinkers, can profess to be both historical and theological.

When we can, we avoid abstractions. Theology can and sometimes must be abstract, since it is concerned with principles and generalizations as well as with those concrete realities from which it takes its point of departure. But an introductory survey of main currents in theological thought should, we think, be as factual as possible, much more so than in deeper, more extensive and specialized treatments of the same matter. This is why we have chosen the narrative form.

3

INTRODUCTION

Patristic theology is the study of the Christian thought of the fathers of the Church.

A "father of the Church" may be defined as an ancient, orthodox, and influential Christian writer.

Naturally, it is often a matter of opinion who is sufficiently influential or who is sufficiently orthodox to count as a father. Even on the question whether certain writers are "ancient" there is serious disagreement. But it has long been customary to date the patristic era from A.D. 100 (Clement of Rome) to the middle of the eighth century (John of Damascus). This seems reasonable enough in view of the fact that before Clement of Rome there were no orthodox, influential Christian writers other than the divinely inspired authors of the New Testament, while after Damascene no Christian writer of undisputed orthodoxy wielded great influence until the ancient Church was a thing of the past.

Each of the first five patristic centuries claims one chapter of the present volume. The sixth, seventh and eighth centuries are treated together in the sixth and last chapter.

Admittedly any division of history into the centuries of our calendar is unnatural, since historical things happen not by centuries, but by periods within centuries or by periods which overlap the turn of a given century. But it is hoped that the beginner in patristic theology will more easily "place" the thinkers and their thought in the period to which they belong if he encounters them century by century. This is the reason

why we have divided our introduction to patristic theology by
centuries instead of by periods, or by currents, or by schools,
or by geographical regions. To make amends, we try always
to identify very clearly the patristic phenomena which "link"
the centuries.

For its compact and handy résumé of the facts of the early
Church history, and often enough for their interpretation, the
author acknowledges his heavy debt to a brief but very
thoughtfully written and challenging work: volume 1 of *The
Christian Centuries: A New History of the Catholic Church*
(New York: McGraw-Hill, 1964). Jean Daniélou has con-
tributed the first section on "The Origins to the End of the
Third Century," and Henri Marrou the second, "The Great
Persecution to the Emergence of Medieval Christianity."
Although the author of this volume has consulted only the
French edition, entitled *Nouvelle histoire de l'Eglise* (Paris:
Editions de Seuil, 1963), references have been added directing
the reader to the appropriate pages of the English translation,
which has been used for citations.

The author wishes to express his humble gratitude to the
recognized scholars of the patristic world who have lent him
their aid, whether across their desks or through their writings.

ROBERT R. BARR, S.J.
Paris, March, 1966

QUESTIONS FOR DISCUSSION

1. What is patristic theology?
2. Define "father of the Church."
3. Which centuries constitute the era of the fathers of the
Church?
4. Express as succinctly as you can any notion you may
presently have of the usefulness of patristic studies for
modern Christian thought. (The same matter will be
proposed for more extended discussion as the last question after the last chapter.)

Chapter 1: The First Century
THE EARLY CHURCH IN NEED
OF LEADERS

In the year 70, Jesus' prophecy was fulfilled: Not a stone was left upon a temple stone; the Romans had razed Jerusalem to its foundations.

And yet the new religion of a few thousand "Christians" (as Antioch to the north had begun to call them) was somehow still alive. This new religion could no longer appear to be just a Jewish heresy, since it was surviving and flourishing when the Hebrew place and nation were no more.

To survive it had to take a whole new turn. We shall follow it in its new turn—in its struggles to free itself from two false messianisms, in favor of a radically new outlook. We shall see it assailed from without, and still more dangerously from within. And for a frightening moment we shall see it without great leaders at the time when its specially delegated founders, the apostles, disappear into history. But then we shall be given reason to believe that great leaders will not be long in coming.

The First Persecutions

In 64 Rome was burned. Nero blamed the Christians, not only because he found them a convenient scapegoat, but probably also so that he might put a halt to the messianic distur-

7

bances of certain Jewish Christian elements that were too rowdy
to suit the taste of the imperial government.

At the very end of the century it was once again a messianism really more Jewish than Christian that occasioned the second important imperial persecution of the Christians, this time
under Domitian.

But if there was trouble from without, there was still
more trouble within. In the first place, Christianity was hesi-
tating between an earthly messianism and the hope of a
heavenly second coming. And besides this, heresies were already arising.

An Earthly Messiah?

For an instant, the infant Church seemed to hesitate between the old and the new. Like a newborn child, the tiny
Church had to learn by groping—by looking everywhere and
reaching for everything. Her divine institution preserved her
from approving error, and even mysteriously guided her groping for truth; but it did not exonerate her from the painful
effort to correctly understand and express (even, at times,
infallibly) the truth committed to her by Jesus. This Church,
the mystical body of Jesus, was utterly perfect and mature as
a divine institution; but she was human as well, and when she
was tiny, when she was just beginning her great human adventure, she grasped at everything, old and new.

The nostalgia for the old was in the South. The thrust towards the new was in the North.

In Palestine and Syria certain Christian groups still dreamt
of what was old and should long since have been abandoned;
they dreamt with Jewish longing (for Jews they were) of the
coming of the earthly kingdom of their Jesus-Messiah. Conservatism has its advantages: It will always know how to
withstand the onslaughts of the radical left, and these particular Syro-Palestinian groups will never know the ravages of
gnosticism. But conservatism is vulnerable on one flank—it
risks being bypassed by the truth. In the year 67, to escape
clashes with the Romans, a Christian group fled Jerusalem
for refuge a few miles north. After the massacre of their

compatriots they returned. And there they sat, waiting for Jesus to come save them with a sword and an army.

A Heavenly Second Coming

Far to the north in "Asia" (today's Turkey), earthly messianism was happily passé. Instead of looking for Jesus to come with an earthly army, they looked for him to come on the clouds of his majesty. Theirs was the pole that triumphed. This is orthodoxy, for Jesus will never come with an earthly army—he will come on the clouds of his majesty, and we look for that coming at the end of time. Progressivism is not bypassed by the truth.

Gnosticism

But progressivism is capable of bypassing the truth, and this is what happened to the hope of a second coming in much of Asia. Christian Asia (today's Turkey) had abandoned Jewish longings for an earthly messianic kingdom to turn its expectations rather to Jesus' glorious second coming. So far, perfect orthodoxy. But decades had passed and he had not come. (What a realistic faith the early Christians had!) Hence now he would never come. How naive—and yet how human. Knowing with the certitude of divine faith that he would come again on the clouds of his majesty, the first generation of Christians watched the skies, expecting him to arrive precisely during their generation (after all, Paul had at first said he was coming soon), and watched in vain. Of this disappointment was born, to those less wise in the Spirit, desperation; and of desperation was born "gnosticism."

Christian gnosticism is the heresy that teaches that some members of the Church live by faith and some by vision. (*Gno-sis* in Greek means "knowledge," as opposed to faith, conjecture, and uncertainty.) It had its roots deep in one form of Judaism, and it contained elements from Iranian dualism and Greek philosophy. The gnostics insisted that a majority of men believe in the mysteries of faith while the elite can see through them. This is heretical because no Christian sees through any Christian mystery. A bishop and a little child live the same supernatural life of faith.

Born of desperation when Jesus failed to come on the clouds of his glory during the lifetime of the first Christians, Christian gnosticism can be characterized by four main traits:

1.   *The God of the Old Testament is an evil god:* he has disappointed our messianic hopes. The Old Testament is to be rejected.
2.   *The visible world is evil:* it is the evil god's creation.
3.   *The God of the Christ is good:* he is completely hidden until revealed in Jesus, who becomes a semi-mythical redeemer of cosmic proportions.
4.   *The spiritual world is good:* it is the creation of the good God revealed in Jesus.

Preludes to Gnosticism. Real gnosticism, complete with all four identifying traits, naturally needed the fall of Jerusalem (A.D. 70) to thrust it into existence, since until then a first-generation glorious coming of Jesus was still plausible. But gnosticizing *tendencies* were in evidence as early as Simon Magus (Acts 8), considered by many or most Samaritans of his time to be himself the good God, who had dethroned the angels that were managing the visible universe so incompetently. Simon Magus is thus the father of gnosticism, for after the fall of Jerusalem his disciples lost hope in Jesus' quick return and became thoroughgoing gnostics, with all four essential traits.

We may mention, as a second early example of the gnostic tendency, the Nicolaitans (Apoc 2:6). They combined the first of the four chief gnostic traits with a moral libertinism.

Real Gnosticism. After the year 70 the disciples of Simon Magus manifest all the essential gnostic traits, in Samaria. In Christian "Asia" real gnosticism is found as a fully developed tendency only towards the end of the century. We see it in Cerinthus and his followers, who combined the four gnostic essentials with the notion that Jesus was born a mere man like other men, and that the Christ did not descend upon him until his baptism in the Jordan. It is interesting to note that Cerinthus is the first gnostic to make perfectly explicit the first of the four traits: He degrades the creator of the visible universe to an evil "demiurge," or world-maker, far inferior to the good God who was to send the Christ upon Jesus.

There are at least a dozen different varieties of pre-gnosticism and gnosticism. But our few examples (the pre-gnostic Simon Magus and the Nicolaitans; the fully gnostic Simonians in Samaria and Cerinthians in "Asia") suffice to point up the essence of the gnostic teaching: The hidden God, manifested in Jesus Christ, is good; hence he is the enemy of Jahweh or any other demiurge, and the enemy of their visible universe.

Engulfed in the gnostic heresy, the tiny Church badly needed great leaders. The evangelist John would live till century's end, but the other apostles had been gone for decades. Will God now raise up "pillars of orthodoxy" (the Greek liturgy's term), learned protagonists of Christian truth, who will bend all the force of their mind and heart and personal magnetism to fight for the majority or the minority (wherever the truth lay)? Orthodox teachers who will fight—win or lose—but who will eventually win, bringing every last heresy down in defeat? "Behold, I am with you all days, even to the consummation of the world": The People of God will have its great leaders, heirs of Abraham and Moses and the strong right arm of the hierarchy; soon they will begin to emerge—the "fathers" of the Church of Jesus Christ.

The First Father of the Church: Clement of Rome

Clement of Rome, who lived in the last half of the first century, writes as the authoritative spokesman of the group of bishops and deacons who governed the Church at Rome in collegiality. Just before the year 100 he wrote a *Letter to the Corinthians*, important precisely for its description of the government of the primitive Church in Rome by a bishop who was recognized as first among the presbyters and chief of the deacons. The letter is also important for its testimony to the Roman martyrdom of Peter and Paul.

The theme of the letter is the unity of the body of Christ through obedience.

Despite the distance between Rome and Corinth, the letter's tone is authoritative. Its author means to be heard. Clement's style is early evidence that orthodox Christianity is to have teachers and guides in her infancy.

QUESTIONS FOR DISCUSSION

1. When were the first two persecutions? What seems to have occasioned them?
2. Where do we find exaggerated Christian conservatism in the late first century, and what form did it take?
3. What was the opposite and symmetrical tendency, and where did it develop?
4. Into what did this latter tendency sometimes develop, and why?
5. What is the central teaching of gnosticism, and why is it heretical?
6. Give the four essential traits of gnosticism.
7. Give one example of a gnosticizing *tendency*.
8. What is the crucial date for the evolution of gnosticizing tendencies into real gnosticism, and why?
9. Give one example of real gnosticism.
10. Who was the first father of the Church? When and what did he write? On what subjects or themes?

Chapter 2: The Second Century
THE EARLY IMPACTS OF
GREEK THOUGHT

In our introduction we remarked that patristic phenomena can scarcely be expected to stop and start with the turn of each century. Naturally each century is linked with the next by a man or men, by a movement or movements. In this first case the link will be gnosticism.

Fully Developed Gnosticism

Satornil is the first great figure of real gnosticism. He is the first to render explicit the natural link between the four main *traits* of gnosticism (reducible to an opposition between spirit and matter) and the *definition* of gnosticism (the doctrine that most Christians live by faith but an elite live by vision). This link he forged by proposing the simple notion that there are two races of men. The elite receive a certain spiritual light from heaven; the many are too material to receive it. Thus the elite are men of the spirit, while the many are men of matter. The unbridgeable chasm between good spirit and bad matter (gnosticism's root notion) is thus responsible for the correlative gap between the elite and the many (gnosticism's definition).

But now something greater than Satornil is about to happen to gnosticism.

13

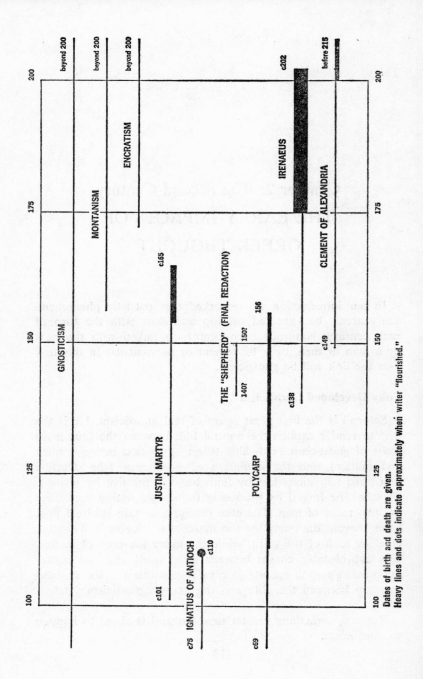

Dates of birth and death are given.
Heavy lines and dots indicate approximately when writer "flourished."

100   125   150   175   200

c75 IGNATIUS OF ANTIOCH
        c110

c69 POLYCARP 156

c101 JUSTIN MARTYR c165

        GNOSTICISM   beyond 200

c138 THE "SHEPHERD" (FINAL REDACTION)
140?   150?   c149

        MONTANISM   beyond 200

        ENCRATISM   beyond 200

                IRENAEUS c202

        CLEMENT OF ALEXANDRIA before 215

The First Impact of Greek Thought

Sown in Christian Asia as well as nearby to the south, gnosticism (1) was promptly hellenized, (2) quickly forked along both Mediterranean shores, and (3) quickly acquired a philosophical foundation. Our reflection will account for the rapidity of these three developments.

These steps are wonderfully logical. (1) A Christian heresy that was really well-rooted in the popular mentality was sure to become "Greek" (hellenized) if all Christianity became "Greek." But indeed all Christianity (except in Syria) was becoming Greek, through the hellenization of the Roman Empire. Hence (2) the gnostics, Greek with the Greeks now, had the ear of vast audiences, and Christian gnosticism spread wildly throughout the hellenized empire. Then, both because of its hellenization and because of the growth that resulted from its hellenization, gnosticism (3) encountered Greek philosophy, especially Plato. And had not Plato proposed a fundamental dualism—a good God and a good ideal world far above the reaches of our shadow-world of sense and matter? The notion was made to order for a gnostic. A gnostic who read the Platonists, as everyone in the schools did, would be startled and enormously encouraged at the similarity between Platonic dualism and gnostic dualism: the radical opposition of bad matter to good spirit.

The mutual respect of gnostic and Platonic dualists for one another was thus both a cause and a result of the westward expansion and Greek intellectualization of the old gnosticism of Asia and Palestine.

Other Heresies and Heretical Tendencies

By mid-century it was no longer gnosticism alone that rocked the Church. There suddenly appeared, as if from nowhere, a half dozen turbulent currents lacking both scriptural foundation and a basis in the traditional spirit of Christianity. They appeared as if from nowhere—that is, they were the spontaneous outburst of an enthusiasm independent of established authority, of an ebullient religiosity untempered by the instinctive sobriety that orientates a calm and collected Christian toward solidarity with the hierarchy. (As a device for the unmasking of heresy, Irenaeus will propose precisely this contrast between the harmony of the teaching of the bishops and the dissonance of the heresiarchs' peculiar ideas; he will picture all the heretics excitedly shouting something different while the hierarchy is calmly chanting in unison.)

It was the rich religious soil of Christian Asia in which the seeds of a heresy took root quickest and most surely. Asia had been the scene of Christianity's most intense religious life since the very decades of the apostles, and would continue as such for centuries. Here Christianity was lived to the hilt: She was at her healthiest when she was orthodox—i.e., when her doctrine was sound—and was most debauched when a magnetic heresiarch would arise. The seat of second-century Christianity's enthusiasm—for better or for worse—was Asia. It is in Asia, then, that we encounter mid-century heresies and heterodoxical tendencies like Montanism and encratism, and heretical personalities like Marcion and Valentinus.

Montanism seems not to have been a dogmatic heresy. At least, it is very difficult to pinpoint any condemned doctrine. Montanism was a Christian fanaticism, an eruption of visions and revelations, women crying warnings, false enthusiasm for martyrdom, fear and hope of calamity for the Roman City of Satan, prophets swearing guarantees that the millennium [1] was already at hand. The Montanists were like the prophets of doom sometimes seen in courthouse squares, crying "Prepare!"

Montanism's cradle was enthusiastic Christian Asia. It originated in mid-century, reached a climax a generation later, and was agitating all Christian Asia at century's end. Then even the prodigious Tertullian, in faraway Rome, would rally to its banner.

Marcion began by taking for his bible only the gospel of Luke and the letters of Paul, thus rejecting the whole Old

---

[1] The expected thousand-year kingdom of Jesus in Jerusalem. Millenarianism is the thought-current which is opposite to gnosticism, which despairs of a second coming altogether. A synonym for millenarianism is chiliasm.

Testament and most of the New. Refused approval at Rome, Marcion went even farther along the road to gnosticism by distinguishing between a "good" God for the New Testament and a "just" God for the Old Testament. Marcion's real talent, however, was not speculative but organizational. His historic feat was to organize a full-fledged gnostic Church (minus the element of despair of a second coming) which was enormously successful.

Valentinus was a gnosticizer like Marcion, but a much deeper thinker. Impressed by an old form of gnosticism called Sethian, in which the Christ descends to earth via seven heavens, taking successively the form of the angels of each heaven, Valentinus evolved a similar doctrine: The Father is utterly above and beyond the reach of all things; but he produces thirty "aeons"; the thirtieth aeon, Wisdom, wanders in quest of her Father with a desire so intense that its reverberations fashion a visible world-prison for our invisible spirits. The Lord then comes down, with a special gnosis for those of us who are spiritual, and we are saved. Here the gnostic disappointment in the second coming, absent in Marcion, is not only present, but is theologized in a fashion which for the spirit of the times is most seductive, and a great temptation for Christians of spiritual depth.

Encratism (from the Greek word meaning "self-controlism") is the doctrine that sex is essentially evil, hence always sinful. The Montanists had taught encratism as a necessary preparation for imminent millennium. Marcion and Valentinus had taught it. (Thus it spanned the opposing poles of millenarianism and gnosticism.) In fact encratism was to be found here and there in many Jewish Christian communities. But in all of these instances it is secondary to another central doctrine. With *Tatian* it becomes the prime essential of Christian life.

Some encratists refused to baptize any but virgins and separated couples. Other encratizers simply baptized the virgins ahead of the other candidates—a custom scarcely reprehensible in itself. But the encratist doctrine that married couples are second-rate Christians was utterly out of keeping with Christian moral principles and naturally provoked bizarre practices.

For example, an encratist ascetic and a young woman would live together in holy virginity, the only species of "marriage" they thought worthy of the Christian calling. It is easy to see that the encratistic notion is a logical consequence of the gnostic condemnation of matter. As one of the most powerful material forces, sex becomes the most thoroughly condemned. When encratism is a product of millenarianism or some other form of false messianism, it represents preparatory self-purification or self-punishment. Unreasonable sexual taboos are a perennial temptation of human religion. They spring from man's unconscious linking of sex and guilt, a link forged in childhood in the selfishness of immature sexuality, and sometimes strengthened later by genuinely guilty, selfish sex. But religion should not condemn sexuality as evil. True religion respects sexuality, and consecrates it.

By the time encratism becomes really strong, it will encounter vigorous orthodox opposition. *Clement of Alexandria* will write at length to destroy the notion that marriage means second-class Christianity. Clement holds that Christian virginity is a higher calling than Christian marriage; but he condemns a virginity that springs from a disdain for marriage. Virginity, says Clement, is no divine vocation unless it is embraced for the love of God.

The First Orthodox Impact of Greek Thought: The "Apologetes"

We must not get the impression that all the thinking and activity of the first Christian decades sprang from heterodoxy. At the end of the first chapter we warned that it was not the gnostics' destiny to march ahead forever unimpeded by orthodox opposition. We have even glimpsed militant orthodoxy in Irenaeus and Clement of Alexandria. Let us turn our whole attention now to the orthodox side of the early Christian conflicts. We shall have our first prolonged look at the fathers of the Church.

If the second-century "apologetes" had been too defensive (too apologetic as we say nowadays) perhaps we would have had in them no Christian contact with Greek thought. But they were never content merely to plead for toleration. They wanted Christianity embraced. And so with all the spontaneity of convinced Christians and loyal Romans, they set out to demonstrate that Christianity was no merely harmless religious phenomenon, but that it contained the very best of all the elements of Roman civilization and empire. Truth is one, the apologetes pointed out. To the mind of a hellenized Roman Christian, then, Christianity and the empire were necessarily ideal soul-mates. If only the empire would awaken to the fact! Far from being subversive, Christians are Rome's most stalwart citizens. Christian thought, far from being irreconcilable with Greek thought, is the best of Greek thought. The "apologies" are full of Homer and the tragedians. Socrates' *logos* was none other than the Word who is God. A genuine Stoic has to be a Christian, otherwise his very Stoicism is incomplete.

Thus Christianity has become intellectual. The Christian-hating philosopher-emperor Marcus Aurelius in the second half of the century is no longer a soldier persecuting an oriental sect, but an intellectual persecuting intellectuals. The philosopher's persecution was, nevertheless, as bloodthirsty as the soldiers', and the apologetes wanted to know the reason why. Was it merely the name "Christian" which brought down the wrath of the empire upon the heads of those who gloried in that name? Indeed it was, claimed the apologetes. Discrimination because of a name was discrimination at its most despicable, and the apologetes saw to it that the whole world became aware of this.

Justin Martyr (fl. ca. 154-165), orthodox Christianity's first theologian, easily surpasses all the other apologetes. If the task of an apologete is to present Christianity not only as the only true religion, but as the only true patriotism, the only true hellenism, the only true philosophy, then Justin Martyr is far and away the champion of them all. Those who came before him (such as Quadratus or Aristides) had not really made very impressive beginnings. Those who came after him (such as Tatian or Athenagoras) paid him the tribute of careful imitation.

Although Justin was born in Palestine, he was born a Greco-Roman pagan. His family was rather well-to-do, and Justin enjoyed the leisure of a rich man's son, the leisure necessary for anyone who intended to study. Justin attaches great importance to his step-by-step progress towards Christianity through his study of philosophy. Restlessly in quest of a wisdom untainted with sham, he recounts his odyssey from one great philosophical school to another until the day he finds the true philosophy in the incarnate Logos, Jesus.

Looking back over the stages of his journey, Justin sees all those other philosophies as one terrible many-headed monster. He disliked his Stoic studies because they avoided problem number one: God. His Aristotelian studies had been progressing reasonably well until one day the professor put out his hand for the customary honorarium, shocking the idealistic pupil: This Aristotelian was much less concerned with truth than he was with tuition. Justin then went to the Pythagoreans. But he disliked his Pythagorean studies because his instructor wanted to fill his head with so much music, astronomy, and geometry that there would scarcely have been room left for the wisdom which Justin sought so ardently. Philosophy would have been just one science among many.

Then Justin came to second-century middle Platonism, and this philosophy was ever so much better. Here was God, the one, the good, the beautiful. Here, too, was God's *logos*. And the inferior world of matter, where a good philosopher could strive for little glimpses of the logos (reason) by constantly purifying his own reason of the body which weighed it down. Justin became a Platonist, and remained a Platonist to his dying day.

Last of all, Justin came to the gospel. Here he found the perfection of Platonism itself. Here the Logos, the Word, was Jesus Christ in the flesh. This, Plato had never suspected! But Justin was struck with the notion that Plato and Socrates (not to mention Moses and Abraham) had all been glimpsing, each in his own so very imperfect way, the source of all philosophy, the Platonic logos, lately revealed as the incarnate Logos in Jesus Christ. In a sense, each of the great thinkers of all times had been a Christian. At long last Justin had discovered the perfect philosophy: Witness the practical visible marvel of Christianity's worldwide expansion, witness the Christians' purity of life, witness their "justice," which, as every Platonist knew, is the absolute prerequisite for knowledge of the Logos. Justin remained a Platonist only because he found Platonism fulfilled in Christianity.

Justin, the Greek philosopher, donned the professor's pallium, and as a new Christian he undertook to propagate the only true philosophy, traveling from place to place and grouping around himself little schools of Christian philosophers. These were the first Christian schools which were not community church-schools. They were philosophical schools in the grand old Greek style, groups of young men gathered around a master who had a reputation for challenging lectures and exciting classroom give-and-take. And especially a reputation for knowing how to embarrass visiting professors.

For his students' sake, one hopes that Justin was not as crushing in the classroom as he was in the imperial court. Your Majesty, he argued, has seen fit to listen to unpatriotic things about Christians. Let the plaintiffs bring forward their evidence. Your Majesty is herewith guaranteed that the Christian community will not protect the guilty, for the Christians are Your Majesty's loyal citizens. And is not Your Majesty praised far and wide for his philosophy, for his culture, for his justice? Excellent—now we shall see whether there is a particle of truth in it! Examine the evidence before you pronounce judgment; otherwise you shall be judged yourself! You can only kill us, you cannot do us harm.

Forthrightness like that was not destined to die in bed. As spokesman for a group of Christians on trial for refusing to sacrifice to the gods, Justin added characteristically that if he were going to die for the truth it would be because his judges, blinded by error, were unworthy of the truth. For that holy folly he was beheaded.

The Apostolic Fathers

When the term was introduced, relatively recently, "apostolic fathers" meant simply the fathers of the sub-apostolic age, the fathers who flourished very shortly after the time of the apostles. One should not imagine a group sitting at the very feet of the apostles. They are rather the half-dozen earliest Christian writers, two or three being anonymous authors of very influential works. The most important of the apostolic fathers are perhaps Clement of Rome, whom we have already seen, Ignatius of Antioch, and Hermas.

Ignatius, Bishop of Antioch (d. 110), during his journey from Syria to be martyred in the Roman arena very early in the century, wrote seven letters to various of his fellow-bishops and their churches. The interest and significance of these letters lies mainly in (1) their anti-millenarianism, (2) their anti-judaizing (the judaizers present an obstacle to the conversion of the gentiles), and (3) their exhortations to the presbyters and their communities to solidarity with the bishops in the face of rivalries which had broken out between the deacons (who belonged directly to the chief bishops of the various dioceses) and the chief bishops' fellow-presbyters. Finally, the letters radiate a remarkable, living consciousness of Christ as savior. Ignatius' love for Christ is so personal and intense that at times the fire breaks right through the rules of written Greek. Indeed, written words, even those of scripture, were of relatively little importance to Ignatius. "To me the official record is Jesus Christ," he wrote to the Philadelphians. "The inviolable record is his cross and his death and his resurrection and the faith of which he is the author. These are the things which, thanks to your prayers, I want to be my justification."

Hermas is author of *The Shepherd,* a collection (completed about 140-150) of visions, allegories, and mandates, recounting the wonderful apparitions of the Christian Church to a herdsman in the fields. The shepherd beheld the Church in all her strength and beauty, older than all the ages, but stronger and more brilliant than any man-made tower. The celebrated image of the stones—her square white stones, her round white stones, the stones taken from streams of water, stones rejected or broken, or worn, or cracked, stones inaccessible among thorns, stones fallen forever in the fire—is found in one of Hermas' long allegories on the classes and orders of the Church. What Hermas is teaching, so readably for the times, is that within (and without) the Church there are many distinct orders or states of life. The milieu is unmistakably Roman, and it is Rome's millenarian drift rather than her gnostic current which colors the writer's Catholic thought.

In another vision Hermas sees the same Christian states of life as "coming" from twelve mountains. From the twelfth and noblest come the holiest and purest of Christians, infants who have never sinned; then the martyrs, the hierarchy,[2] the true and charitable Christians, the rich and worldly, the hypocrites. Finally the apostates, whose sin can never be remitted.

The second century is also the age of the eminently readable and often reliable *Acts of the Martyrs*, records of the victims' Christian testimony, their judicial processes and eventual martyrdom. Especially is it the century of the martyrdom of the nonagenarian *Polycarp* (fl. ca. 112-156), bishop of Smyrna. It is the century of the great surge of New Testament apocrypha, and other Christian writings in prose and verse. Interesting as they are, we cannot examine them, for they are not central to Christian theology. Awaiting our attention is the greatest Christian of the century.

Irenaeus, Greek Bishop of Gaul

The only episcopal see in Gaul in the second century was that of Lyons. The populace of the whole region spoke or understood Greek, the language of the empire; it was not inappropriate, then, for a priest who had come to them from Smyrna, in Asia, to be selected bishop.

Whereas Justin the philosopher had written towards mid-

[2] Bishops and presbyters, missioners, deacons; and virgins or widows consecrated to a life of charity.

Another "order" or state at the time seems to have been that of prophet, to which the author, Hermas, must have belonged.

century for the pagans, *Irenaeus* (fl. ca. 175-202), a biblical scholar, wrote towards the century's end for believers. He has been described as the first systematic Christian theologian, though his work is, on the whole, more properly called catechetical.

The great need of second-century believers was an antignostic polemic, and in Irenaeus they found their champion.

We have already seen how Irenaeus criticizes heretics in general for their disunity, contrasting it with orthodox harmony. Against the gnostics he urges the same criticism; only he does so more forcefully. Are the heretical sects out of tune with the hierarchy, and even discordant among themselves? Then the worst of them, the gnostics, easily outdo all the others—gnostic theology *is* disunity. Their Old Testament god of creation is the enemy of the God of redemption.

Unity, then, is Irenaeus' central thought: In the beginning came creation; then the redemption; now men await the second coming.[3] All fuse together in a single coherent movement planned by the one God before all ages.

Unity—this is what Irenaeus is proud of. If he gloried in the fact that he taught only what was taught by his fellow bishops, who had all together received it from the apostles, he gloried as well in the fact that he had known Polycarp, who had known the apostles. His justifiable pride in this unbroken chain of unity with the apostles stems from his view of a bishop's sacred office: to hand down the doctrine of the apostles as pure as it was when the apostles taught it themselves. And Irenaeus knew how to hand it down in all its exciting richness.

Creation, redemption, second coming—one thrust towards

[3] Irenaeus was a millenarianist, the most obvious thing for an antignostic to be. Gnosticism denied a second coming; millenarianism said the second coming would be tomorrow. Millenarianism is at the opposite pole from gnosticism. Since the second coming is of faith, gnosticism is heretical; but faith knows nothing about this time of the second coming, hence millenarianism is not heretical. And for a Christian who lived only a few generations after Jesus, it seemed plausible enough that he might come tomorrow. (After all, Paul had specified that the Lord would not delay, and the Apocalypse ends with the cry "Come, Lord Jesus!" Other millenarians: Justin, Hermas, Tertullian, Origen, Hippolytus.) Irenaeus even interceded in Rome on one occasion in favor of the Montanists!

man's complete restoration in Christ, towards his "deification" [4] in the beatific vision: "God's glory is a living man—and man's life is to see God," wrote Irenaeus.

The Impact of Alexandria

Egypt must have had Christian missioners right from the beginning, even if they are unknown to us because *The Acts of the Apostles* and the letters of the New Testament deal only with the expansion north and northwest. The earliest evidence of Christian influence in Alexandria links Alexandria directly with Palestine and Jerusalem, not with the later communities of Asia or Greece. Cerinthus, whom we have seen working in Asia, eventually came to Alexandria; and there in the second century a certain Carpocrates developed some Cerinthian ideas into a gnosticism which recalls Asian gnosticism in its most radical form. The gnosticism of the Alexandrian Basilides is in the Palestinian tradition of Simon Magus, but it is Syrian at the same time. So we can see that gnostic influence at Alexandria was both early and extensive. Thus currents from all the earliest Christian communities met in Alexandria. These currents were heterodox as well as orthodox. But most significant for Christianity was the impact of Greek thought encountered in Alexandria.

Alexandria was a city both hellenized and cosmopolitan. Here, too, Christianity will become hellenist. It may be that the first Christian missioners in Egypt were already strongly influenced by Greek culture; certainly, by the time the second century is well under way, Alexandria at the mouth of the Nile is the most hellenized crossroads in the Mediterranean world. A second-century Alexandrian was so accustomed to being surrounded by foreigners that he tended to take them for granted. The cosmopolitan, liberal-minded population of Alexandria provided a ready market for another foreign import, Christianity, in both its orthodox and its gnostic manifestations. And the great metropolis in turn changed the Chris-

[4] See below, chapters 4 (Athanasius) and 6 (The End of the Patristic Era).

tian cultural mentality from Jewish to Greek, just as it had swallowed up everything else that came to its shores and inevitably hellenized it. The stage was set for "the Christian hellenism that will be the miracle of human history." [5]

Clement of Alexandria (fl. ca. 200-215) is our principal source for the history of Alexandrian Christianity during the period of this hellenization. He was the first great teacher of the catechetical school there. This institution was to become a sort of Catholic university and easily the outstanding Christian school of the time. Clement's work in connection with this enterprise won for him the title "Father of the Church."

Clement is not the first Alexandrian to combine Greek thinking with biblical revelation. Philo the Jew had done so, if too rationalistically, with the Old Testament; and Pantaenus, Clement's predecessor in the school, had made the attempt with the New Testament. But Clement was the first father of the Church to do so. Like Justin, he combined Christianity with the Platonism of his time.

Perhaps no father of the Church has been subjected to judgments as varied as those passed upon Clement of Alexandria. He bears the title of "Saint" no longer. It is often very difficult to discern precisely what he taught, for he preferred discussion to conclusions. In later centuries his disciples tended to heterodoxy, which, of course, rendered Clement suspect in the view of later writers—perhaps without good reason. He was probably not a priest. Indeed, he esteemed the clerical state less than did other fathers. Before Clement, Christian biblical study stressed the parallels between the Old and New Testaments, like that between David the king and Christ the king. Justin, Irenaeus, Tertullian, and Hippolytus are representatives of this Palestinian tradition.

But things take a quite different turn in Egypt's hellenized metropolis. To the Old Testament, as a forerunner of the New Testament, will be joined a second herald: Greek culture and even Greek mythology. Philo had already introduced Alexandrian Judaism to the notion that secular learning and culture must be brought into the service of biblical exegesis.

[5] Daniélou, p. 159; cf. Eng. tr., p. 128.

He had even included music, astronomy, and number-symbolism. The Christian Pantaenus doubtlessly moved along the same lines. Now the latter's pupil and successor, Clement, is to propagate it in the influential catechetical school, and to emphasize philosophy. In other words, Clement proposes that in order to understand the salvation announced in the New Testament, the New Testament has to be studied not only in the light of the Old, but also with the help of mythology, science, philosophy, and all Greek culture.

To the student who perseveres, Clement promises a promotion: He will pass from the naive faith of the many to a gnosis granted only to a few. Was this a *gnostic* gnosis? Very likely not. Clement's gnosis seems to be genuine supernatural faith. It is no penetration of, no seeing clear through, Christian mysteries. Clement's gnosis is simply faith which has become a higher faith, faith which has passed into a more reflective certitude, the fruit of long and patient application to the secular sciences. Unlike the faith of the many, Clement's gnosis is a scientific faith. Like the faith of the many, it is a supernatural faith, a free gift of God. For Clement, faith comes to the individual, and is received personally; it enters into the warp and woof of each man's existential actuality and experience. Clement's gnosis is the reward granted to those among the faithful who laboriously apply the findings of the human sciences to the divine heritage of revelation.

Let us take a concrete example. David is a "figure," a "type" of Christ, not only because David was king of Israel and Christ is king of Israel, but also because David composed the psalms, sang the praises of God, as Christ was one day to offer to his Father the only perfect praise. But was David the only psalmist before Christ? Was not Orpheus also a psalmist? Did not Orpheus, too, compose and sing the most spellbinding musical poetry on the highest themes, to the accompaniment of his lyre? Thus in the view of Clement of Alexandria, Orpheus joins David as "figure," or "type" of Christ.

Clement appears to have been the first to introduce to Christianity a theory of divinely inspired pagan Greeks. Justin had claimed for them glimpses of the Logos, but with Clement there is question of real inspiration, something akin to biblical inspiration. According to Clement, the more ancient pagans received an inspiration of great intensity, while pagans of succeeding ages gradually lost the divine fire until it was nearly extinguished. Then suddenly Christ came with all his plenitude of divine truth. Thus Homer (or our Orpheus) would be greater than, say, Socrates or Plato, since the older the pagan sage the more fully he participated in divine inspiration, and the fuller his insight into the Logos or divine Reason. In other words, an originally elevated pagan philosophy gradually degenerated through the ages, until it was finally restored to its perfection by Christ.

Justin had seen Christianity as having the answers to the most vexing philosophical questions. But with Clement, the perfect wisdom of Christianity becomes the property of Alexandria, the crossroads of the world. How important this will be for the history of Christian thought!

QUESTIONS FOR DISCUSSION

1. What Christian phenomenon overlaps the first and second centuries?
2. Who is gnosticism's first great figure, and what is his main contribution?
3. Why did gnosticism spread so quickly?
4. What do gnosticism and second-century Platonism have in common?
5. Describe Montanism. Where did it originate? What special quality of this locale favored its birth there?
6. Was Marcion Montanist or gnostic? Give the reason for your answer. For what is he most to be remembered?
7. Recall the doctrine of Valentinus the gnostic.
8. Describe encratism. Does it fit gnosticism? Does it fit millenarianism? What father of the Church is its outstanding enemy? What is his line of attack?
9. What is the aim of the apologetes? What is their line of attack?

10. Who is the greatest apologete? Recount his step-by-step progress towards Christianity. In what element, central to Platonism as well as to Christianity, does he link Platonism and Christianity?
11. How did Justin go about propagating his doctrine?
12. How did Justin die?
13. What is the meaning of the term, "apostolic father"?
14. What is the teaching of Ignatius of Antioch?
15. Describe the content and form of the doctrine of the *Shepherd* of Hermas.
16. Who is the first great nemesis of gnosticism? What is his line of attack?
17. Did Christianity come to Alexandria early or late? Where did it come from? Was early Alexandrian Christianity heterodox or orthodox?
18. What is the most important thing that happened to Christianity at Alexandria? Name the two qualities of Alexandria that favored this phenomenon. Link each with the phenomenon.
19. Who was the first great leader of the Alexandrian catechetical school? What is his main contribution to Christian thought?
20. Describe the theory of Clement of Alexandria concerning the divine inipration of the ancient pagans.
21. Compare, then contrast, Clement's gnosis with heretical gnosticism.

FURTHER PROBLEMS

1. How are Montanism or encratism (or how is millenarianism in general) opposite to gnosticism?
2. Are all encratistic tendencies dead and gone in your own Christian milieu? If yes, how long have they been dead? If no, are they weaker than they were, say, a generation ago?
3. Are baptized infants who have never sinned holier and purer than adult Christians?

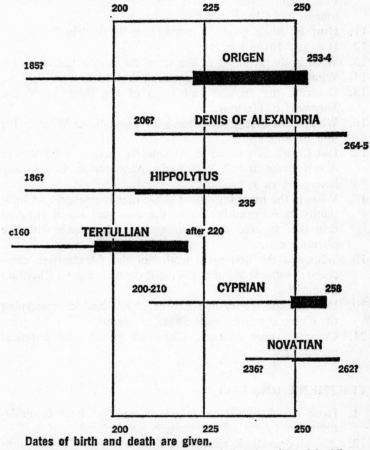

Dates of birth and death are given.
Heavy lines indicate approximately when writer "flourished."

Chapter 3: The Third Century

Plato Christianus

The patristic link between the second and third centuries
is the hellenism of Alexandria, so crucial for the history
of Christianity. A Christianity dominated by Jewish mores
and a Jewish mentality is now a thing of the past.

Neo-Platonism

Plato Christianus is the classic expression for Platonic
Christian thought; it is as though the great philosopher himself had been baptized right along with his philosophy. The
phrase applies to the "middle Platonism" of the second century, which we have met in Justin and in Clement, but it applies most of all to the Christian neo-Platonism of the third
century. The neo-Platonism of the third century, like the
middle Platonism of the second, fell sadly short of the greatness of the real Plato in the quality of its insight into reality.
But neo-Platonism was still great; it was the most important
Greek philosophical movement after the second century, the
last great movement in ancient thought. It was based on
what was left of Plato in the third century. As *the* critical
hellenistic influence on Christianity, it deserves attentive
examination.

Neo-Platonism originated at Alexandria, in Christian
form with Origen and in pagan form with Plotinus. Both Ori-

gin and Plotinus had as their master one Ammonius Saccas, about whom we know very little. He was, however, through his students, the link between the middle Platonism of the second century and the neo-Platonism of the third. As the reader was reminded in our introduction, there are really no currents of thought, there are only currents of thinkers. Thus, neo-Platonism is best seen in the great neo-Platonists. Our own examination of the current will be focused around its Christian founder, Origen.

A Giant among the Fathers

Origen (fl. ca. 222-254) started to read the bible at such an early age, and he read it so attentively and reflectively, that at the age of eighteen he was ready to head the Alexandrian catechetical school when Clement left the city during the persecution at the dawn of the century.

Not merely a child prodigy, Origen is one of Christianity's half-dozen greatest luminaries. Compared with him, earlier fathers were like candles. None of them, not even the Platonists, had dared to venture beyond the frontiers of strictly biblical thought. Origen constituted in his person *the* great impact of Greek thought on Christianity, thereby profoundly influencing Christian theology for all subsequent history.

Origen's path to knowledge was the reverse of that of his master Clement. Born a Christian, Origen found Christ first and Plato later.

Platonism as Origen understood it could be sketched somewhat as follows: Utterly above and beyond all things, especially beyond all multiplicity, and altogether inaccessible to creatures, God the Father freely generates a Son. This Son seems somehow inferior to the Father and yet he is the same God since he is God's perfect image. He is identified with Plato's logos. Because he is Plato's logos, and because he is the image of the Father and the same God as the Father, the Son is beyond multiplicity and accessibility in his *being*. Nevertheless he is not beyond *functional* contact with an inferior world, for through him the Father creates an infinite world of pure spirits, who are to live forever in a state of ineffable joy and happiness; their only task is to love and be loved. But they are endowed with free will, hence they can choose to love less, or not love at all. Love cools in some, and for punishment and purification they are imprisoned in bodies more or less gross in proportion to the distance of their fall from the primordial intensity of their love. Least fallen (and thus inhabiting the airiest bodies) are the good angels. Farthest fallen, in the heaviest, most repulsive bodies, are the demons. The reader will recognize instantly the third class of bodies, the in-between bodies whose spirits still love a little: bodies such as our own.

Now, the logos who mediated the creation of the spirits will pay their ransom. He will come in Christ for their restoration. By Christ's grace all [1] will eventually succeed in the painful ascent towards the bodiless purity of their first state of love and joy. This concept will make Origen one of the great theoreticians of asceticism, as well as of trinitarian and Christological dogma. The ardent Alexandrian is propagating a teaching designed to impel his disciples to prayer, to holiness, and if possible to martyrdom.

There are of course many doctrinal errors here, and these represent but a few of the theological excursions. The massive influence of such a genius on later Christian thought was not always sound and healthy. The modern ascetical notion of the human body as an evil thing comes down to us from Origen through Evagrius, and through writers dependent on Evagrius like the Abbot Cassian, and finally through the modern ascetical school which cited the disciples of Evagrius with approval. Yet far from being a heretic, a man consciously at odds with the dogma of the Church, Origen

[1] Even the demons. After all, any spirit is a person, and for Origen a person bereft of free choice would no longer be a person. But free choice, Origen argues, implies the possibility of a change of choice, hence the possibility (in God's providence, the certainty) of the conversion of the demons. (Unfortunately, in Origen this means that our restoration to bodiless purity need not be definitive, since spirits are eternally free to fall again and again! Origen lacked the concept of a free will in heaven or in hell so irrevocably committed to the supreme good or to the supreme evil it has embraced as to be no longer capable of a change of choice.)

firmly asserted his intention of holding to Christian doctrine without the slightest deviation. And we have to grant this, that his speculations on an eternally generated Son, and his theology of a divine Spirit, represent for the times—anterior by a hundred years to the era of the great early ecumenical councils—a daring progress toward a patristic explicitation of the New Testament dogma of the Trinity.

To understand Origen and the daring of his thought, one must glance at some of the events in his life.

Origen was in his adolescence at the beginning of the century when Emperor Septimius Severus struck out at the Alexandrian catechists and their catechumens. The edict evoking the persecution had been directed specifically against Christian proselytism; thus it was the candidates and their instructors who bore its brunt, while long-time Christians were left alone.

One wonders what sort of a teen-ager Origen would have been today. The greater the number of catechists struck down, the more pupils the completely fearless Origen welcomed to his own class. As more and more catechists were sent off to prison, more and more frequently Origen was at their side— in prison, in court, at executions, publicly encouraging them every step of the way at the risk of his life. The great *Eusebius of Caesarea* (fl. 318-339), "the Father of Church History," [2] tells us that this young Alexandrian found it exhilarating to risk danger and death for Christ. One is tempted to believe the story of Origen bidding his mother farewell because he expected on the morrow to join the ranks of the martyrs. After a tearful embrace they retired for the night, but his mother took care to hide his clothes. And so Origen was forced to save his life in order to preserve his dignity, and the Roman state was deprived of a martyr that day.

When Origen was seventeen, his father was added to the list of martyrs and Origen was able to continue his studies only because a charitable lady undertook financial responsibility for his family. So many catechists had fled with their master Clement that the bishop of Alexandria confided the whole Alex-

[2] Noted as well for his extremely important role in the history of Arianism, which we sketch in chapter 4.

andrian catechetical system to Origen. Confronted with a classroom of Greek heretics and philosophers, Origen quickly decided that he was going to have to become a philosopher himself. Postponing much of his catechizing, Origen put himself under the tutelage of Ammonius Saccas, and soon became the father of Christian neo-Platonism. He converted the catechetical school into a kind of academy, or Catholic university, where all subjects were taught, but all were taught only for the sake of theology. He was the first Christian to achieve genuine intellectual recognition, the first to compel the respect of even the most competent scholarly adversaries.

We are told that Origen's writings numbered in the thousands. Seven stenographers operating in relays, seven longhand copyists, and enough young ladies to turn it all out in calligraphy, made up the team put at his disposal by a wealthy benefactor in an endeavor to keep up with his lectures and dictation.[3] It was his inexhaustible energy that earned him the somewhat indelicate (for our times) nickname "Bowels of Brass" (*Chalchenteros*)—"Man of Steel," let us say. Pagan kings and governors, an empress, heretics and crowds of Christian orthodox were to be found in his numberless audiences.

Not all, however, fell under Origen's spell. There was the case, for instance, of the local bishop. Just at the time when the school was enjoying its greatest influence and was, therefore, the most jealous of its academic freedom, Alexandria had a bishop, Demetrius, who was just as concerned about his own influence. He was busy extending it into the dioceses beyond his own metropolis throughout the flatlands of Egypt in the ever-widening sphere that was to be one day the patriarchate of Alexandria. Demetrius naturally looked askance at this dazzling independence right on his own doorstep. And so, it seems, he attempted to take control of the school.

Origen would have preferred not to rebel, but he felt that there were certain insights into Christian truth which could only be the fruit of long and deep theological reflection on the bible, insights which were not necessarily meant to be handed

[3] Eusebius, *Ecclesiastical History* 6.23.1.

down via an apostolic succession of unscholarly bishops—
men who had not, after all, been exposed to the long and profound theological training of Origen's school. The task of
the bishop was to transmit the traditional biblical, apostolic
deposit of faith, not its theological elaborations. By what
right, therefore, could he interfere with the school of theology?

Perhaps Origen was partly right, but perhaps, too, he was
partly gnostic. Like Clement of Alexandria, Origen held to
the distinction between a supernatural faith common to all
Christians, and a gnosis attained by only a few through theological speculation on what is of faith. So far this can be perfectly orthodox. Yet Origen may have been in trouble with his
bishop, not just over some aspect of the school but over the
very principle of ecclesiastical supervision of Christian education. One wonders, then, whether his particular gnosis was altogether free of a heretical gnostic exclusivism, and whether
Origen may have felt that the educated Christian elite had a
faculty of "seeing through," be it ever so little, the mysteries
of the Christian faith—that the elite possessed a knowledge
the rest of the faithful, bishops included, are denied.

However history may one day answer the question of Origen's orthodox or heterodox gnosis, his bishop's answer was
simple. Demetrius assembled an episcopal synod and drove
Origen from Alexandria. It was in Palestine that the exile chose
to reopen his school, and he was received with open arms
(as he was everywhere else—at Rome, Athens, and the
other great centers), despite the pleas the Palestinian bishops
were receiving from their Alexandrian colleague. Origen re-
opened his school with full ecclesiastical approbation.

Only when he was in his sixties was it granted to Origen
to fulfill his teen-age ambition for martyrdom. Decius had
just brutally closed the first peaceful fifty years of the third
century with a persecution that reached to all corners of the
empire. So in mid-century the fiery old world-champion of philosophy and theology was tortured so cruelly that he never
recovered. Mercifully he died a very few years later.

In loyal Christian style, Origen had based his neo-Platonic

theology on the bible so that most of his writings fall in the category of exegesis. His approach was astonishingly painstaking and scholarly. For his own use, he composed a six-column Old Testament: one column for the Hebrew, one for the Hebrew in Greek letters, and four columns for the Septuagint and three other Greek translations. Where the translations differed from the Hebrew, he used the customary marginal signs to show where and how they differed. Sometimes he proposed his own textual emendations.[4] He journeyed to the Holy Land, dug in the caves, interviewed the rabbis, and attempted to situate geographically every biblical place name for which there was the slightest traditional evidence. He added a seventh, or an eighth, or a ninth column to his bible where he found interesting new readings, for there had been new manuscript "finds" in his time, as in our own.

Yet for all the scientific values in his approach, an allegorical interpretation of the bible was normative. For Origen the bible was not what it is for us today, the history of salvation narrated by God himself in the words and notions of human authors, the "witness," the profession of faith of the People of God. For Origen the bible was "a sea of mysteries." Every event, every name, every etymology, every numeral, had been secretly and directly invested by God with a hidden meaning unknown even to the human author. This meaning it was the task of the exegete to "discover." No corner of metaphysics, morality, philosophy, or science could escape the conclusions Origen draws from every jot and tittle of the sacred text.

To the mentality of our generation the method seems without reason or foundation, but it was hard to refute! A relatively orthodox allegorist (like Origen) was usually possessed of a Christian sense that would prevent him from simply transgressing all conceivable bounds, yet would leave him free to find anything orthodox anywhere at all in the bible. Put the bible into the hands of a genius already in control of a complete, self-consistent, preconceived system of philo-

---

[4] Origen's emendations were consulted with great interest and respect a century later by Jerome, when the latter was composing the Latin Vulgate.

sophical theology—Origen has no equal among the fathers for method and synthesis—and what will an allegorical biblical exegesis deliver, but the exegete's own complete, self-consistent, preconceived system? Thus, utterly free of internal contradiction, and endowed with the weighty precedents of hellenistic philology and of the bible itself (e.g., the allegory on Melchizedek in the letter to the Hebrews), Origen's allegorism stood impregnable for centuries.

In fact, the literal sense of the bible shocked and embarrassed him. The patriarchs had lived with many women, while a Greek pagan would live with only one. And so on and on. (The pagans and the gnostics loved to remind orthodox Christians that pagan Greek morality was more "reasonable" than that of the Old Testament.)

"It is deeply moving to note with what energy and earnestness this great and devoted scholar dedicates the work of a lifetime to fathoming the truth of his one ardently loved book, firmly convinced that he is on the way to penetrating ever more deeply into its content, while in fact he remains the prisoner of the assumptions of his Platonizing and gnosticizing philosophy, incapable even of seeing what separates him from the Old and New Testaments." [5]

But this great and devoted scholar did his work with such spellbinding perfection that his successors made the name of Alexandria synonymous with biblical allegorism for hundreds of years, a biblical allegorism which endured among spiritual writers even to the twentieth century. He had, besides, a sense of the transcendence of the divine message, a divine whole greater in its scope and depth than the sum of its human parts, a transcendence that had to wait for twentieth-century biblical theologians to be rediscovered.

Heresies and Heretical Tendencies

Denis of Alexandria (fl. ca. 233-265), the most remarkable representative of that outstanding generation of Eastern bish-

[5] H. F. von Campenhausen, *Fathers of the Greek Church* (New York: Pantheon, 1959), pp. 50-51.

ops formed in the school of Origen, naturally shared his master's neo-Platonic doctrine of the Trinity. In Origen, this doctrine looks clearly "subordinationist": In relegating the Son to an intermediate state of being between the inaccessible Father and the Father's creation, Origen seems clearly to have subordinated the Son to the Father as second-class God.[6] In Denis, this subordination is, happily, not so clear. Denis insists, at any rate, that he is not a subordinationist. Still, he laid stern emphasis upon the distinction between the being of the Father and the being of the Son in order to counterbalance the opposite tendency (the oneness of the divine nature) which certain Western theologians were exaggerating to heretical proportions.

In the West, the dogma of the oneness of the divine nature had reduced the distinction among the divine Persons to a merely apparent distinction, so that the "three" Persons were only three "modes," three manifestations, three facets of the one divine nature—no longer three really distinct Persons. This Western heresy is called "modalism" (or "Sabellianism," after Sabellius, its champion at Rome). This heretical over-simplification of the three-in-one (in favor of the one to the detriment of the three) is a natural reaction of human rationalism in the face of the greatest of Christian mysteries. All trinitarian heresies have emerged from an attempt of the tiny human mind to squeeze out from under the awful weight of the mystery of the three-in-oneness of God. Modalism (Sabellianism), which holds that there is really only the one, which presents itself *as if* it were three, was a Western tendency. This evoked in the East a counter-tendency stressing the real distinction of the three Persons.[7]

6 Even if it is true, as is likely, that Origen was clearly subordinationist, it is nevertheless wise to keep in mind that in Origen as in so many other early fathers, a distinction is to be made between his faith and his theology, between what he believes and his frequently imperfect efforts to understand and express what he believes.

7 In our own twentieth century there have been Eastern Orthodox theologians who accuse the Roman Catholic Church of teaching that God is first and foremost one nature, and that if he is three Persons as well, it is only because the three Persons flow from the one nature. No, say these Orthodox, God is neither one first nor three first; he is simulta-

The task of the counter-stress on the trinity of Persons [8]
naturally fell to the bishop of Alexandria, chief hierarch of the
East. As Origen's pupil, Denis was well molded for the task.
Origen before him had *too much* distinguished the Father from
the Logos, so that the Son was God in a secondary way—subordinationism. Denis insists that he himself does not want to
go so far. He insists that he in no way *separates* the Father
from his perfect image, the Son, even if in *distinguishing* them
he rejects the word "consubstantial" because it smacks of
unity of person; [9] and if he called the Son a "something-made"
by the Father he only meant that the Father generates the Son.
Denis will not admit for a moment that his terminology, so
startling when reported in the West, betrayed a heterodox theology. Perhaps we should agree with him. There was not much
fixed terminology in his day. He provided a fine Eastern counter-
stress to the Western heresy, modalism. On the other hand, his
theology does look somewhat subordinationist, even taking
into account the nuances of the Greek language which he in-
vokes in his defense. Interestingly, Denis' defense under attack looks much more orthodox than the writings attacked!

Who, by the way, had attacked? Rome, of course. To Rome,
the Alexandrian bishop sounded like an out-and-out heretic,
with his denial of "consubstantiality" and his statement that
the Son is "something-made." In the West, "consubstantiality"
meant oneness in nature,[10] and was therefore correctly applied
to the Son. "Something-made," on the other hand, could in the

---

neously three-one. Or perhaps it is even closer to the truth to say that
he is three first, and that the oneness of his nature flows from his being
three. "First," "flow," and "simultaneously" here refer not of course to
time, but to the eternal, timeless *structure* of the Trinity, as also in
Catholic theological terminology.

[8] Denis' healthy counter-stress will go too far one day in the East. The
divine Persons would no longer be merely *distinct,* but *separated,* so that
the Son would not be one in nature with the Father. This would entail
the denial of full divinity to the Son—subordinationism—the Arian explosion of chapter 4, below.

[9] "Consubstantial" had to wait a hundred and fifty years to be defined
in ecumenical council as referring to identity of nature, not of person. In
the third century, especially in the Greek language, it could have just as
easily meant identity of person—precisely the modalistic heresy.

[10] Tertullian's term (See below).

West denote only a creature, hence could not be applied to God the Son. One can no more blame Rome for her suspicion than Denis for his Greek words. Denis was condemned by a Roman synod that sat under the presidency of the pope.

As bishop of the great metropolis of Egypt, Denis might have neglected the condemnation with impunity. But Denis is very significant for his eagerness—we know it from his letters—to maintain the closest possible solidarity with other local churches, especially with Rome. This is why he is quite ready to defend himself against the Roman condemnation, even though he is so powerful and so far away.

Modalism was not all Denis of Alexandria had to combat. There was also millenarianism, the doctrine that the second glorious coming was already at hand. Origen had been a millenarian, especially in his youth. Justin, we saw, had been a millenarian. In fact, until now most of the fathers had been millenarians, including Denis' contemporaries Tertullian and Hippolytus (see below). But Denis was as doggedly set against it as we are today. He even went so far as to reject the apostle John's authorship of the Apocalypse, which, with its theme of woe to the City of this world and "Come, Lord Jesus!" was one of the sources of millenarianism.

The Birth of Latin Theology (1): The West in Travail

Except for Irenaeus of Lyons, a transported Asian, there is no great theologian west of Egypt before the third century. But that century is scarcely under way when Western theology rises up with a suddenness and a vitality that presage a glorious future.

As in the East, where Christian thought was born in the throes of gnosticism (A.D. 100), it was born now in the West (A.D. 200) in comparable agony. Only, the enemy here was millenarianism.

We have left Origen, Denis, and their Eastern neo-Platonism in mid-century. Now we retreat fifty years to retrace the same decades in the West. The transition will be easy, for *Hippolytus of Rome* (fl. 206-235) belonged to the same conservative, millenarian milieu that Denis would fight two generations later in Alexandria, the sluggish current that would not flow on with the mainstream of Christian thought. More specifically, millenarianism was a reactionary mentality, incapable of resigning itself to the reality of a Church which would live on in this bad old world for a long time before Jesus would return again. Montanism had just reached Italy and "Africa." [11] And Montanism—the eerie propheticism of our last chapter —was millenarian. This meant an Italy and an Africa infested with a radical religious conservativism dead set against any compromise with the City of Satan (the imperial government). Why weaken at the last moment, when Jesus is coming tomorrow? This in turn meant enthusiasm for martyrdom,[12] and martyrdom has always been recognized as one of the marks of authentic Christianity. Thus Montanism (along with other millenarianisms) could present itself as authentic Christianity. A storm of apocryphal Acts of the apostles, *Acts of Peter* (*"Quo vadis? To Rome to be crucified"*), *Acts of Paul and Thecla, Acts of Martyrs*—exalting martyrdom, encratism, and female prophecy—present all the special traits of Montanism. Why soldier for the empire—indeed why even bear children—when the end of the world is tomorrow? At our distance of 70 generations it is easy to shake our heads at the millenarian naiveté. But in the year 200, there were a good many sincere and fervent Christian millenarians.[13] Had it not been for the hierarchy, eternally circumspect, ever slow to move, immune to fanaticism, above all prudent—and therefore prudently anx-

[11] The patristic term for the region around Carthage; today's northern Tunisia and northeastern Algeria.

Recall from chapter 2 that by the beginning of our third century, Montanism was to have infested all Asia and to have come even to Rome (See discussion of Tertullian, below).

[12] Millenarianism's uncompromising opposition to the programs of the State (it was anti-marriage just when an emperor was endeavoring to rebuild corrupt Roman family life, it was pro-desertion just when the barbarians were first daring to assault the farthest military outposts of the empire) provoked the assault on Christian proselytism which so aroused the enthusiasm of the youthful millenarian Origen.

[13] Including most of the fathers of the Church. For example, Origen, Irenaeus, Tertullian, Hippolytus.

ious for good relations with the empire just when Christianity was beginning to emerge from its ghetto—who knows whether the roaring millenarian minority might not have swallowed up much of Christianity and then died of its own foolishness when Jesus delayed in coming. But it was not for nothing that Jesus had founded a hierarchical Church, and it was the position taken by the bishops against millenarianism that caused its slow death.

As in the case of Origen and his bishop, here, too, it was a question of a forward-looking Church authority versus entrenched private theology. But now it was much clearer who was innocent and who was guilty. At Rome it was an out-and-out case of a violently reactionary private theologian against a moderately progressive hierarch, and it was tooth and nail. Hippolytus stopped at nothing short of direct assault on the episcopal authority. Invective is the word for it. Violently he denounced Pope Zephyrinus for Sabellian modalism, and then denounced that pope's oracle and successor Callixtus for moral laxity in absolving too easily from sins against purity and for forgiving the unforgivable sin of apostasy.

At first, there may have been something in the charge of modalism. Zephyrinus and Callixtus were administrators, not theologians, and Sabellius was a quiet, peaceful heretic. But once the modalistic danger became really clear, Callixtus condemned Sabellius. Hippolytus was caught by surprise and was even more angry than before!

Hippolytus lived 15 years after the death of his enemy Callixtus. Thus his twenty years spent fighting popes are nicely redeemed by nearly as many amiable years, during which he cooperated closely with Callixtus' successors. He wrote extensively. His numerous exegetical works, in striking contrast to the writings of Alexandrian allegorism,[14] are typically Roman, catechetical and liturgical. He died for the faith in the mines of Sardinia, together with Pope Pontianus, who had become his personal friend.

Hippolytus of Rome made a serious mistake in which he

[14] See the discussion of Origen, above.

persisted for twenty years. He refused to look upon the Church of Christ as she really is—as the wheat growing with the tares described in Jesus' parable, good and bad Christians living side by side till death and judgment. He mocked Callixtus' inspired image of the Church as Noah's ark, filled with all manner of noble and ignoble living creature. Hippolytus' Church was a dream-church, a minority clique of saints in conflict with the world,[15] poor and despised, every one of them following Jesus with unfaltering step, clear to Golgotha. He was rigidly opposed to hierarchical centralization, that is, to the monarchical non-collegial concept of diocesan administration. For it was precisely the chief bishop of each diocese who, as pastor of the one lost sheep as well as of the ninety-nine in the fold, would be inclined to fight Hippolytus' concept of the Church as a sect of saints. Times changed, and Hippolytus was left in the dust of history. Hippolytus fought for the retention of the Greek language when the whole Western Church wanted Latin. He was a reactionary in an era when the Church had just chosen to be progressive. He was integralist when the hierarchy was for adaptation. We may thank God that Callixtus was there as pope during Hippolytus' twenty years in the dark.

And yet, we may thank God for Hippolytus, too: saint,

---

[15] The Church will always be in conflict with "the world"—that "world" for which Christ did not pray (Jn 17:9). In the midst of their very opposition to Hippolytus, the hierarchy, as they became less and less minoritarian in mentality and the Church became more and more respected in Roman society, were actually becoming stricter and stricter where the "world" had made inroads incompatible with genuine Christian moral standards. They were increasingly severe on indirect cooperation with idolatry, for example, the interior decoration then in vogue in pagan private homes, or on such dishonest business practices as having two prices, practices that a Christian might have been inclined to go along with in the course of Roman daily living. Today it would probably be cheating "a little" on income tax. We shall always have to fight the "world."

But what about that other "world," the world that Christ came to save, not to condemn (Jn 3:17)? Is it not one of the tasks of the Church in the world to serve the world? The twentieth-century hierarchy is still having to put us on our guard against the second- and third-century sect-mentality of a Hippolytus, and to remind us that the world for which Christ did not pray and against which the "Church militant" is supposed to militate is "not against flesh and blood, but principalities and powers"; error and sin, not other Christians.

father of the Church and martyr, and personification of Christian fervor and dedication to the death.

The Birth of Latin Theology (2): Tertullian

The first great figure in Western Christian thought, *Tertullian* (fl. ca. 196-221) was born and raised a pagan, became a Christian at about the age of 40 and died a Montanist. By now the reader must be thoroughly convinced of the allure of millenarianism for early Christians.

It was the ageless Christian miracle of martyrdom that won Tertullian to the faith (and possibly to the priesthood) at the turn of the century. Every one of us has been struck with the fact that converts often tend to be the most intransigent, the most uncompromising, the most conservative, loyal, and faithful of Christians. This was eminently the case with the great Tertullian, whose conversion had been occasioned precisely by the heroism of martyrdom—that supreme uncompromise where a Christian lays down his life for his friend. From the very year of his conversion he became the Christian apostle of intransigence, and a mere decade later he was so struck with the unyielding spirit of Montanism in Rome that he became a Montanist himself. (Montanism presented itself precisely as the party of martyrdom; millenarianism always promoted martyrdom. If there was no persecution, there were millenarians who would provoke one. Burning to death in small groups today, they felt, was scarcely much more terrible than burning to death with the whole world tomorrow in the last conflagration.) He is the probable author of the beautiful *Acts of Perpetua and Felicity,* telling of their martyrdom.

Montanism had just arrived in Rome after some fifty years in Asia, and Tertullian was to be its foremost protagonist in Christian Africa. The city of this world could go to hell: Tertullian's martyr-sect of encratists, doctrinaire teetotalers and conscientious objectors, awaiting the second coming, would have no part of it. With a Tertullian on their hands (as earlier with a Hippolytus) what could the hierarchy say in answer to accusations that a good Christian was a bad Roman?

Tertullian also joined in Hippolytus' attacks on the easy absolu-
tions of Pope Callixtus and criticized the *Shepherd of Hermas*
on the same grounds.

But it is for none of this that Tertullian is most remarkable.
He was not the first Montanist; he was one of the last. He was
not the first African Christian; Christians had been there for
a hundred years. It is the genuinely original Christian theology
Tertullian built in Africa that makes him remarkable as the
very founder of Western Christian thought.

Before Tertullian, the Christians of Carthage spoke Latin, but
their culture was Greek. Hence the theological currents of their
metropolis came from the East (if sometimes via Rome).
Under Tertullian's influence, on the contrary, African theology
was to become Latin to its very core, leaving behind in its
thoroughgoing latinization even cosmopolitan Rome and her
cosmopolitan hellenism. Let us see what Tertullian's new
theology would be.

Its most striking trait, judging at first glance, is its vocabulary. Tertullian refused to translate Greek theological terms. He
created them in Latin. He was using *consubstantialis* (of one
substance) long before the Greeks had their corresponding
term, *homoousios*.

But at second glance, what is more significant about Tertullian's authentic Latin vocabulary is its juridical tone. In Rome
Tertullian had been a lawyer of renown, and now in Africa
he commandeered a host of legal terms, endowed them with
a theological content, and employed them to batter the hapless
heretics with an argumentation whose every loophole was foreseen and plugged. His spearhead was what in law is called
"prescription." Tertullian's Christian application of "prescription" could be summarized somewhat as follows:

Marcion and other heretics are bringing suit against the
Church of the bishops for possession of the correct interpretation of the scriptures. But the bishops' churches include those
which were founded by apostles. And these apostolic churches,
indeed the Church of the bishops as a whole, are unanimous
against the heretics in their interpretation of the scriptures.
This direct historical connection of the Church of the bishops

with the apostles, whom Christ taught, plus her unanimity in interpreting the scriptures, demands a verdict against the heretics, according to the principle of Roman law that *prior and uninterrupted possession of goods* constitutes just possession of those goods. Therefore, Tertullian argued, let the heretics abandon forthwith their claim to read the bible more accurately than the bishops. This is excellent courtroom procedure, and one can visualize the discomfiture of the poor heretics, who had never thought of theology as law.

In Tertullian God becomes legislator and judge. God lays down a law, and judges transgressors. Found guilty, the defendants must pay the penalty—unless, after voluntarily entering a plea of guilty and appealing to the clemency of the court, they undertake to counterbalance the gravity of the penalty with an equal weight of virtuous actions. Some virtuous actions are commanded, others recommended; it is by the latter that the condemned pay their penalty.

Does this sound familiar? It very well might, for a legalistic approach to broad areas of theology has remained characteristic of the Christian West since Tertullian inaugurated it in broad areas of his own theology in 200.[16] Before then, and in the East even since then, such an approach was practically unheard of because it was unthought of.

Two other important remarks about Tertullian: as a philosopher he tends to Stoicism, without being shackled by it; and, like Clement of Alexandria and Origen, he considers profane sciences and philosophy necessary for a study of the Christian faith.

[16] It has been asserted that Tertullian's *thought* about God and man is not nearly so legalistic as his *terminology,* a terminology natural to a lawyer. His real terminological preoccupation, we are told, is not with juridicism, but clarity and precision.

If this be true, then the West has not always done well by him, for our legalistic theological tendencies, which are scarcely always purely terminological, were first set in motion by Tertullian's legal terminology. A juridical approach in some areas of theology is legitimate; but in the West it has sometimes become a theological mentality.

Whatever may have been Tertullian's intentions when he wrote, he wrote so well that he is *de facto* if not *de jure* the father of Western theology.

The Battles of Cyprian of Carthage

It was just mid-century when Emperor Decius decreed that, in token of loyalty to the empire, his every subject would personally and publicly burn incense to the immortal gods of Rome. Each would then receive a certificate to testify that he had acquitted himself of that duty. The incense-burning was to be far more a display of patriotism than an act of idolatry. But idolatry it was, because it was looked upon as a religious as well as a civil act. This put the Christians in an agonizing dilemma. Many a heretofore "good Christian" unceremoniously tossed a few patriotic grains on the coals, nervously shifted into the adjoining line to collect his certificate, and left feeling very guilty. Many another stealthily bypassed the incense queue to whisper to the certificator: Could he really not arrange to seal a certificate right away? The other line was very long, and the petitioner was quite pressed for time. And many another paid for his faith with his blood.

When the crisis was past, the certificate holders, incense-burners or not, swarmed to the Church for absolution. What was she to do? Treat them as apostates? There were clergy who never absolved apostasy at all, while even the hierarchy at large imposed a long and heavy penance. What to do with these least of apostates, the certificate holders?

The radical right knew what to do. Send them into the outer darkness with mortal sin on their soul. But for the hierarchy, charged by Christ with the care of the lost sheep, the answer was not quite so simple. Most of the hierarchy absolved, after long and heavy penances.

In favor of this latter solution was *Cyprian* (fl. 249-258), Bishop of Carthage, a writer both prolific and profound, and a father and doctor of the Church. The celebrated intervention of those who had not yielded—the confessors—in favor of those who had yielded—the "apostates"—weighed heavily with Cyprian. Cyprian decided to absolve (after severe penances). But he would not undertake to do so without the consent of Rome. He wrote Rome for her approval to absolve the "apostates."

The Roman see was vacant at mid-century, precisely as a result of the recent persecution. The *locum tenens*, the leading presbyter of Rome, replied that Cyprian would have to await a Roman synod and the election of a Roman bishop for a definitive answer. (Of course, he could absolve in imminent danger of death.) That *locum tenens* was *Novatian* (fl. ca. 249-262), who was privately merciless toward the certificate holders.

But to Novatian's dismay, the bishop Rome elected was Cornelius, who forthwith approved Cyprian's plans for clemency at Carthage. Whereupon Novatian rebelled, had himself consecrated bishop, went into schism, forbade absolution of the "apostates," and proselytized all corners of the Mediterranean. Novatian's church was like that of Hippolytus a few decades before—a dream-church of martyrs and virgins and saints.

The legitimate hierarchy was altogether in favor of martyrs and virgins and saints. But the Christian Church is a Church of sinners too. There was indeed a place for the "Christian elite," the religious state, in which one strove to die to the world and, so far as possible, to die to sin through a very rigorous asceticism. In the world, however, one exhorted the Christian not to sin, and afforded him the support of the sacraments; he sinned anyhow, of course, but when he was truly repentant the Church absolved him in the name of Christ, imposing a penance proportioned to the gravity of the offense. Because of orthodoxy's toleration of repentant sinners, within a year's time Christian Rome's first great Latin writer, Novatian, was condemned. It was at such a price that Cyprian's liberality was vindicated. The West was surely suffering a painful beginning in Novatian, as earlier in Tertullian.

This most edifying and encouraging hands-across-the-sea was not to last long. On penance there was total episcopal accord. But in a new quarrel the bishops of Rome and Carthage were to be found on different sides. This time it was baptism. A heretic's baptism, held Cyprian of Carthage, is invalid because a heretic has denied the true faith, while baptism is precisely the sacrament of initiation into the true faith.

Stephen of Rome, on the contrary, forbade the rebaptism of heretics, thereby implying that baptism administered by a heretic can be valid.

The reader knows who prevailed. The practice of the Church today remains that of Stephen of Rome. There is but one baptism, that instituted by Christ, and whoever baptizes as Christ intends, baptizes validly.

Cyprian's about-face unsettles us when we reflect that his reason for inquiring into Rome's position on the absolution of apostates could not have been merely to win expected support for his own decision to absolve the certificate-bearers. That support was not a foregone conclusion. The Roman see was vacant, and had Novatian, the man in power during the interregnum, been elected pope, he would have rejected Cyprian's position. Cyprian could not have been sure beforehand that he would receive a favorable reply. Cyprian's reason for writing to Rome was quite honestly that he recognized Rome's jurisdiction over Carthage in the matter of the absolution of the certificate-bearers.

But in the baptism question, Cyprian rejected Rome's interference. Did Cyprian hold Rome's right to intervene in the affairs of another local church, or did he not? The answer seems to be: Yes, he did. But only in interdiocesan questions:

> It is clear that Cyprian's thought contains an ambiguity on this point; or, more exactly, he stands at the junction of two movements, to both of which he bears witness, but whose reconciliation he does not foresee. He is attached to the unity of the universal Church and in particular to the primacy of Rome, but he is also well aware of the rights of the local episcopate. Stephen on his side appears fully aware of his right to intervene in the affairs of other Churches, and Cyprian also recognizes this right. . . .

If, over and above particular questions, we try to discover the significance of the controversy, we realize its importance. It concerns the principle and modalities of the primacy of Rome. The primacy itself is not in dispute; Cyprian is one of its great upholders. What is in dispute is its extent. What Cyprian declines to accept is intervention in a field which seems to him to depend on the prerogatives of the local Church; he is sure that the violence of Stephen's condemnation reveals a tendency on the part of the bishop of Rome to abuse his authority. But to the extent that dogma was involved, Stephen was acting lawfully in asserting his right to intervene. As the future will show, he was right. Deeper insight made it possible to solve the problem. But the dangers of particularism on the one hand, and of authoritarianism on the other, can already be foreseen in this great debate.[17]

Let us conclude chapter 3 with the risky attempt to recapitulate third-century Christian thought in two swift strokes of the brush. Western theology (like its father Tertullian) is new: Latin and juridical, with Stoic philosophical tendencies. The East remains old: Greek, mystical, and Platonic.

QUESTIONS FOR DISCUSSION

1. What patristic phenomenon links the second and third centuries?
2. Which is the greater philosophy, Plato's (fourth century B.C.) or neo-Platonism (third century A.D.)?
3. What is the name of the last great movement in ancient thought?
4. Which two disciples of a single teacher founded it?
5. What was the first service Origen performed for the Church?
6. Which, if any, fathers before Origen match his stature?
7. Sketch the great "Origenist myth" that so influenced Christian neo-Platonism.
8. What second service did Origen render to the Church?
9. Origen's third service to the Church was to undertake the study of philosophy. What was his motivation?

[17] Daniélou, pp. 201-202.

10. Did world scholarship esteem Origen during his lifetime?
11. What became of Clement's catechetical school at Alexandria under Origen?
12. Did Origen write much?
13. Why did Origen transfer his school to Palestine?
14. How and when did Origen die?
15. Describe Origen's remarkable preliminary textual and archaeological work with the bible.
16. Contrast our modern attitude toward the bible with that of Origen.
17. Bishop Denis of Alexandria may be thought of as a kind of link between Origen and Arius, since Arius, like Origen, is to teach at Alexandria that the Son is inferior to the Father. In what two key expressions of Denis did Rome think she found evidence of this "subordinationism"? How did Denis defend himself?
18. It may not be clear whether Denis is really a subordinationist, but it is clear why he felt he must write in terms that look subordinationist. Explain his motivation.
19. Eastern patristic theology originated around A.D. 100 in the throes of the gnostic struggle. When was Western patrology born, and what thought-current caused pangs to the Church at its birth? Describe this thought-current.
20. Describe Hippolytus of Rome's attack on the popes.
21. Who was the first great father of the Western Church?
22. He was an extremist. How? Why?
23. Why is Tertullian considered the founder of Western Christian thought?
24. What element of Tertullian's theology or terminology has been the most enduring? Give an example.
25. Describe sin and salvation à la Tertullian.
26. Identify the "certificate holders." How did Cyprian of Carthage and his fellow bishops tend to deal with them?
27. Why did Christian Rome's first great Latin writer quit the Church?
28. On the question of the certificate holders, Cyprian, bishop of Carthage, stood with Rome. But on another question

he resisted Rome's interference. Describe this latter quarrel.

29. What seems to have been Cyprian's criterion for deciding when to obey Rome and when not to?
30. Can you capsulize the state of Eastern and Western theology in the year 300?

FURTHER PROBLEMS

1. What was bad and what was good about Origen's biblical allegorism?
2. "The pope is infallible when pronouncing *ex cathedra* on faith or morals," and he enjoys genuine jurisdiction over the whole Catholic Church. Then how can it be that good men like Cyprian, in the foremost centers of Christian thought, struggle with a pope?

Chapter 4: The Fourth Century
THE ZENITH

Often between one century and the next there flows a strong continuous current, moving like a flood over the centennial dividing-wall. We find it strange that there is no such current here. There is no notably strong carry-over of doctrine, event, or personality from the third century into the fourth. As we enter this greatest of patristic centuries, the theological sea is calm.

A fisherman learns, however, to sense in a certain gentle breeze a calm somehow too fresh not to be ominous, a calm that heralds wind and lightning. It may be that we, too, in our journey through the patristic centuries, should be capable of apprehending in the gentlest of fresh theological breezes (from Alexandria—if there was to be a link between the centuries it would still be Alexandria) something a shade too fresh, something disquieting. Perhaps we should know that we are on the threshold of a terrifying storm. But it is too early for the body of Jesus Christ, the Christian Church still in her theological infancy, young and inexperienced and childlike, to know.

So it is the year 300, and the theological sea is calm. None of the great fathers is yet alive except Athanasius and he is still at his mother's knee.

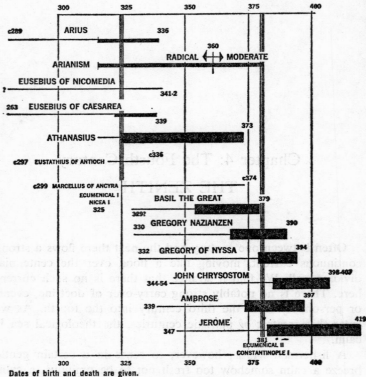

Dates of birth and death are given.
Heavy lines indicate approximately when writer "flourished."

Thunder on the Left: Arius of Alexandria

Thunder in the distance used to be a reliable token of good fortune or misfortune on the high seas. If it thundered on the right, fine sailing was in store. But if it thundered on the left, the voyage proceeded at the risk of the sailors' lives. The same was true for the Church in the fourth century.

Smoldering uneasily side by side in the Church of Alexandria for long decades, two radically immiscible tendencies tolerated one another only because they had never really confronted each other. The episode of Denis of Alexandria [1] had

_____
[1] Recall chapter 3, above.

been a narrow escape. A glance back at our account will remind the reader what these tendencies were: (1) subordinationism, and (2) a theology of full equality between Son and Father. After a handsome dressing-down from the bishop of Rome, Denis had kept the uneasy peace by an adroit retreat from subordinationism to equality.

But two generations later, early in our fourth century, what was bound to happen occurred. The irresistible force met the immovable object, head on.

Christian truth is a uniquely precious gift that inspires in the authentic Christian sacred love and fear. Instinctively, he feels it to be something altogether too delicate and fragile for rough handling. Because its content is the Infinite whereas the intellect to which it is confided is finite, man can never wrap it all around. He dares not attempt to reduce its dimensions to packageable size by simplification. A careless touch will misshape this gift. Above all, an attempt to force it into its finite package will break it to pieces.

The noblest example is the doctrine of the Trinity. Christianity proclaims a paradoxical God, who is one in being three and three in being one, and one not in spite of being three but, mysteriously, because of being three, and three not in spite of being one but, mysteriously, because of being one. This is the first and greatest mystery of faith. Lay a heavy hand on this precious and delicate truth and you become a modalist (like Sabellius). Or a tritheist. Or an atheist.

Christian doctrine affirms another precious and delicate truth. All reality comes forth from God the Father: the other divine Persons and all creation. From the Father comes the Son, in a begetting more perfect than creaturely begetting. From the Father comes the Holy Spirit, in a procession through the Son which has no creaturely analogy. From the Father together with the Son and the Spirit comes the world, in a coming-forth from nothing: creation. Nothing exists, divine or creaturely, which does not come forth in some way from the Father.

But not everything comes forth in the same way. All reality is brought forth by the Father, but *not everything is brought forth from the same point of departure:* the Son and the Spirit come forth *from the Person of the Father* in a begetting and a procession, but all other things are brought forth *from nothing* in a creating.

Deeply impressed with the basic truth that all things, even the Son, come forth from the Father, *Arius* (fl. ca. 318-336), priest of Alexandria, was not at all impressed with the *delicacy* of that truth. He concluded that the Son was created. For Arius, all manner of coming forth was to be imagined as one form or another of being created. Since he could not visualize a production which was not a creation, he refused to admit an uncreated Son. And so it came about that Arius began to teach that the Son was somehow inferior to the Father, that he was the first and most perfect of creatures, since the Son's begetting must be somehow a creating. A creation "before all the ages," doubtless, and inconceivably nobler than the creation of the immaterial and material world. But still merely a creation.[2]

Some have found a quality of psychological obsession in Arius' excited discovery and preoccupation. But at the root of every plausible error (every error that anyone believes), there is a scintilla of truth. In Arius' very error there is a hidden truth: The Son and the world do both come forth from the Father. This is orthodox Christian teaching. But in reducing all coming-forth to being-created, Arius was reducing the co-equal Son to the status of creature, ignoring this Son's own "I and the Father are one" and thereby departing from Christian orthodoxy.

This was clear subordinationism.

Alexandrian bishops, long masters of the cluster of dioceses around their metropolis, enjoyed the unquestioning obedience of scores of other bishops. An Alexandrian metropolitan, then,

[2] The confusion Arius stirred up by centering all his premises on "unbegotten" as the exclusive property of the Father was scarcely clarified by the near identity in Greek between "unbegotten" (*agennetos*) and "not become" (*agenetos*), especially when Arius called into the theological arena the man on the street who, besides not being a theologian, did not always distinguish between the single *n* and the double *n* in his speech!

was utterly unprepared to tolerate obstinacy on the part of a simple priest of his own diocese. When Arius refused to be silenced, the archbishop, Alexander, with a hundred of his suffragan bishops, excommunicated him without ado (318). But Arius had friends in Palestine and "Asia," fellow alumni from days gone by. Many of them had become influential bishops, and enough of these proved their loyalty to Arius by declaring for his subordinationism. Thus, despite a flurry of letters from Alexander to Rome and to bishops everywhere else, Arius found episcopal protection in Palestine and Asia. Whereupon the bishops of rival sees in the same region, whether or not they had given the question much reflection before now, instantly steeled themselves in their orthodoxy. So Arius had mustered to his cause, among others, Nicomedia in Asia, and Caesarea in Palestine. Suddenly facing these for a fight were the bishops of Ancyra, Antioch, and Jerusalem. The torches were lit for a conflagration.

The First Ecumenical Council: Nicaea (325)

Constantine himself felt this to be a situation which threatened the unity of the Roman empire, reunified under his scepter only months before, and he had a truly imperial thought: an ecumenical council.

There had never been an ecumenical council. There had been the council of the apostles at Jerusalem (Acts 15) and countless local and regional councils since, presided over by the metropolitan hierarch of the region, like the Alexandrian synod that had just condemned Arius. But there had never been an "ecumenical" council, a council of the bishops of the whole "world," a Christian plenary synod of the Roman Mediterranean world. But if there had never been an ecumenical council, neither had there ever been such a threat to the peace of the whole Church and the whole empire; nor indeed had there ever been a Christian emperor [3] who would be personally con-

---

[3] Constantine was baptized only on his deathbed. It was a widespread custom of his day, and even later, to delay baptism until maturity, until the sins of one's youth were past. (A better known example of delayed baptism is Augustine of Hippo.) The practice arose primarily from the

cerned with the religious life of his Christian subjects. There
had never been an ecumenical council, but the time was surely
opportune. Constantine convoked the First Council of Nicaea
in the northwest corner of today's Turkey.[4]

The majority needed to condemn Arius was easy to muster:

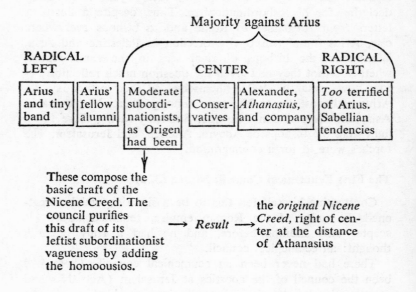

Majority against Arius

RADICAL LEFT		CENTER			RADICAL RIGHT
Arius and tiny band	Arius' fellow alumni	Moderate subordinationists, as Origen had been	Conservatives	Alexander, *Athanasius,* and company	*Too* terrified of Arius. Sabellian tendencies

These compose the
basic draft of the
Nicene Creed. The
council purifies
this draft of its
leftist subordinationist
vagueness by adding
the homoousios.

⟶ *Result* ⟶ the *original Nicene Creed,* right of center at the distance of Athanasius

---

seriousness with which any catechumen (to say nothing of an emperor
who was responsible for the murder of his relatives) might take future
Christian obligations. Despite his postponed (and Arian) baptism, then,
Constantine is to be considered a Christian emperor because he was a
convinced Christian personally (we know not how deeply).

[4] Constantine did what lay in his power to make Nicaea ecumenical,
not only in principle (he invited all the bishops of the world), but also
in fact (he put the imperial post-dispatch at their disposal). But fourth-
century Western Europe was simply too far from Asia geographically. Of
the 300 fathers of the first ecumenical council only three or four came
from the West. The pope was represented by legates, setting a common
precedent.

In the words of Marrou:

We can picture the different theological tendencies in the council [of Nicaea] like an open fan. At the extreme left lay the small hard core of the first Arians, supported by their Sylloukianist friends [their fellow alumni, i.e., disciples of Lucian of Antioch], grouped around Eusebius of Nicomedia. Next came a sort of left center, whose spokesman was Eusebius of Caesarea, grouping the moderate subordinationists in the tradition of Origen with those who could be called conservatives. The conservatives were composed of uncertain or timid theologians (a similar tendency will be found more than once in later councils) more concerned for unity than for precise definitions and hence hostile to all new formulas; they tried to hold on to traditional teaching expressed in strictly biblical terms. Further to the right were those who had discovered the danger of Arianism: Alexander of Alexandria (accompanied by his deacon and future successor, Athanasius) and Hosius of Cordova, who seems to have played a specially active role. They were supported by an extreme right wing, whose backing they seemed to consider free from danger: Eustathius of Antioch and especially Marcellus of Ancyra. The latter in particular was all the more violently anti-Arian in that his passionate, one-sided devotion to the principle of divine "monarchy" led him to veer into the diametrically opposite heresy. His enemies seem to have been correct in attributing to him an acknowledged or implicit modalism, the old error of Sabellius.

This analysis does not bring out the relative importance of the different parties. In fact, a powerful majority easily took shape to disapprove of the errors of Arius. Disregarding the protests of the "conservatives," the council took as its basis the profession of faith proposed by Eusebius of Caesarea, but added to his rather vague text certain very precise definitions. Not content with proclaiming the Son "God of God, Light of Light," they [the council] expressly stated that he is true God of true God, engendered and not created, consubstantial with his Father, *homoousios.*

The adoption of this word [*homoousios*], in defense of which severe battles were later to be fought, marks a memorable date in the doctrinal history of Christianity. By thus inserting in the profession of faith a new term which originated no longer in scripture but in man's reason, the Council of Nicaea recognized as fruitful the purely theological attempt at elucidating revelation, and used its authority to sanction the progress made in rendering explicit the contents of faith.[5]

The universal Church for the first time made a dogmatic "definition." The universal Church officially and formally started down the one-way street marked "evolution of dogma."[6]

The Church and the Emperor: Caesaropapism?

It is hardly likely that Constantine was a competent theologian. Yet he not only convoked Nicaea; he must have hurried it, perhaps even guided its discussions. It went surprisingly well. Once the decisions of the council were taken, he bent all the force of his ruthless imperial might that they be accepted everywhere by everyone. The precedent was to be followed regularly by other Christian emperors until the fall of the empire itself in the fifteenth century.

Caesaropapism is too strong a word to describe the relationship of the fourth-century emperor to the Church. The

[5] Marrou, *Christian Centuries* I, p. 252.

Homoousios, a philosophical word, is not used at Nicaea in a philosophical sense. This is, in fact, the genius of Nicaea, that it does not canonize a philosophy. It defines that "because the Son is *from* what the Father is, the Son *is* what the Father is." Cf. John C. Murray, *The Problem of God* (New Haven: Yale, 1964).

[6] "Evolution" in the sense of "homogeneous development." The Church proposes new dogmas; i.e., infallibly guaranteed (though not necessarily perfect) formulations of divine revelation. It does not discover any new revelation, but does come to a progressively deeper and more meaningful consciousness in faith of the message revealed in Christ and delivered to the apostles.

Roman empire was indeed a totalitarian state, and a police state. Beginning with Valentinian (fl. 364-375), a Christian emperor would roast to death over a slow fire not just an assassin, but even a recalcitrant draft-dodger. In the civil sphere the emperor was omnipotent. And he interfered in Church affairs as well (sometimes as ruthlessly as in civil matters). But it was not as would-be heads of the Church that the new line of Christian emperors interfered in her affairs; it was as her eldest son and protector. True, this eldest son and protector had something of the divine about him; he was God's legate for governing in the civil sphere and protecting in the ecclesiastical sphere. But as a member of the Church he was a subject of the hierarchy, at least in principle. Though Theodosius the Great (fl. 379-395) was to manage a reprisal-massacre of 7000 people in the arena of Thessalonica over the protests of the bishop Ambrose—a mortal sin but a civil matter—Ambrose would manage to impose a public penance on the almighty sinner. True, this new brand of Roman emperor is much more powerful in Church affairs than his later counterpart, the "secular arm" in the Middle Ages which will carry out the Church's crusades, heretic-burning, council-enforcement, and all her "temporal affairs." Our patristic-age emperors are exercising ecclesiastical power. They are convoking the councils, determing the subject matter for their deliberations, marshaling their majorities. But they are less than head of the Church. Sacred head of the holy Christian empire, yes; but not pope. New Moses, new David, yes; but not new Peter.

Thunder on the Right: Athanasius of Alexandria

Young deacon at Nicaea, old lion of the homoousios for two generations, bishop of Alexandria exiled five times by four Arian emperors, *Athanasius* (fl. 325-373) is far the greatest of the anti-Arians and far the greatest father of the first half of the fourth century, the indefatigable and violent champion of Nicaea through half a century of anti-Arian controversy, eventual negotiator of the Arian return to orthodoxy. His writings enjoyed enormous appreciation and wide publication, especially after his lifetime.

Against the Arians, condemned but not convinced at Nicaea, Athanasius' tack was that the "Joannine" Logos,[7] the Son, had to be homoousios, consubstantial with the Father, because only an incarnate God could restore fallen man to the primeval image of God. Man really died when Adam sinned—otherwise God's warning that death would result from tasting of the forbidden fruit would have proved empty bluster, says Athanasius. And once the divine image is killed in man, it takes a man who is God to restore it. Athanasius' (and, in fact, the whole East's) concept of man's divine life, lost in Adam and restored in Christ, is just that realistic. "The Word of God became man," wrote Athanasius, "that we might become God." This is his clinching argument: If God did not become man, man cannot become God. A participated deification, as the supernatural, existential destiny of human nature, is so inextricably rooted in the spiritual theology of the whole East by Athanasius' time that he can offhandedly appeal to it as the unsupported major premise of his argument for the full divinity of the divinizer, the redeemer.[8] Surely, God might have remitted man's *guilt* by simply magnanimously pardoning it, without the incarnation of the consubstantial Son; but man's *corruption* would have remained—the divine image would not have been restored. The modern Western idea that God has perfect freedom to restore man by a kind of general amnesty, with no need for a divine savior to make full satisfaction for the infinite offense (recall lawyer Tertullian), would have struck both Athanasius and his Arian adversaries as anthropomorphic and juridical. Is God to grant amnesties like an offended terrestrial monarch, who deigns to pardon instead

[7] Athanasius writes as if his logos-theology were that of the fourth gospel. In reality his logos is more neo-Platonic than biblical.

[8] Only implicit in its biblical roots, the Eastern doctrine of man's deification had gradually become more explicit in Justin, Irenaeus, Clement of Alexandria, Hippolytus, and Methodius of Olympus. Becoming clearer and clearer step by step throughout two centuries, it had become so explicit that Athanasius could thus appeal to it without any discussion of it. See below, chapter 6.

of punish? And was the fall primarily an "offense," a juridical affair capable of being pardoned? Or was the fall not primarily the privation of a reality, the image of God? [9] The image of God, a real entity, was part and parcel of man's concrete creation in grace. And it was *genuinely divine life*. Once lost, it needed to be rebuilt by a new creation in a man who is God. So argues Athanasius of Alexandria against the Arians. Nicene orthodoxy, soon to be the almost exclusive property of the West for two generations, is to have a champion in the Arian East. Orthodoxy was still alive in the East, despite Eastern afterthoughts about Nicaea.

Scruples in the East: The Scandal of the Homoousios

Roman Catholicism and Eastern Orthodoxy exist side by side today in a state of schism. The causes of the schism are multiple, complex, and imperfectly known even to the scholars of the schism. Its history is long, extremely involved, and generally post-patristic. But it has its roots in the Arian controversy and the dogmatic definitions of the Council of Nicaea. For it was with Nicaea that East and West first ceased to understand one another.

Homoousios, meaning the Son's "consubstantiality" with the Father, turned out to be simply unacceptable in the East.

In the West, Tertullian's "consubstantial" had for a hundred years meant what it means to us today, i.e., that the Son is unambiguously one in essence with the Father, without compromise of the distinction of their Persons. But in fourth-century Greek translation, "consubstantial" was extremely suspicious. In the first place, homoousios had a materialistic tone. Two coins of the same substance, say two silver coins, were *homoousia*—consubstantial.

In the second place, *ousia* was not a Greek word for "substance." *Ousia* simply meant "being." Therefore *homo-ousios* meant merely "one in being." And now all of a sudden at Nicaea homoousios is to mean "consubstantial," "one in sub-

---

[9] The image theme will be taken up specifically in subsequent booklets of this series.

stance." Who had decided this? Who had narrowed the meaning of ousia from "being" to "substance," so that homoousios was no longer vaguely to denote identity of being, but very precisely to denote identity of substance? Who had decided that homoousios would denote *identity of substance to the exclusion of the heretical identity of person?* (After all, persons are "beings" at least as much as substances are.) Who had narrowed down the meaning of the Greek word homoousios at Nicaea? The West—the Latin West, scarcely represented at Nicaea? The West, cradle of the Sabellian "one-in-Person" heresy?

To put it bluntly, who had inserted the homoousios at Nicaea to "purify" the Eastern schema? [10] The invisibly present West, whose soldier-emperor Constantine had brought the East to her knees only six months before. The West, mother of Sabellian modalism.

Hence we should not be surprised to find, after Nicaea, some Eastern afterthoughts. The Greek bishops knew what *they* had meant when they signed their names to the Nicene homoousios. They had meant what they (rightly) believed the West meant: identity of substance, not the heretical identity of person. But now they began to wonder about that Nicene homoousios. The word itself means "one in being." If by "one in being" the Nicene homoousios meant only that the Son is one in essence and substance with the Father, well and good: This is what the East had taken it to mean when she signed it. This is orthodoxy. But if by "one in being" the Nicene homoousios meant that the Father and Son are also one in Person (the Sabellian heresy)—if so much as an ounce, even a grain, of the "one in Person" notion had been smuggled in by the West in a first shipment of the detested modalistic heresy— then the East was ready to withdraw its signatures. As if enough Sabellianism had not just been discovered at Ancyra itself! In a word, the East was afraid.

A dogma of conciliar infallibility had not yet been elaborated. The West had provided a fertile culture of Sabellianism a good hundred years before, and Western theology still in-

[10] See chart of Nicaea, above.

nocently harbored strains of the virus which it would take her another twenty years to recognize. Recognize it she would, and reject it. But that happy moment had not yet arrived. Athanasius of Alexandria and the whole West with him could go right ahead with their emphatic assurance that the homoousios was only consubstantiality and not Sabellian modalism. But who was to guarantee the truth of these assurances? The West which did not detect the Sabellian germs in its system?

We see how imprudent it would have been—or how imprudent they decided it would be [11]—for the Greek-speaking bishops to remain the homoousians they had become at the Council of Nicaea. A fact is a fact: In the Greek theological language of the fourth century "homoousios" *could* have been the perfect term for Sabellian modalism.

So they withdrew their signatures. One by one most of the Eastern hierarchy let it be known that they no longer professed the Nicene homoousios.

If the reader is beginning to think that the Arian controversy has become a complex affair, we have to remind him sorrowfully that "complex" is a relative term. Never in the history of the Church has there been an affair more complex and confused than the history of Arianism yet to come, the twisting trail from Nicaea I to Constantinople I, from 325 to 381.

If we were to set out to really tell this story we would risk having to change the title of our booklet to "The Arian Controversy and Certain Other Patristic Phenomena," double its size, and tempt the reader to put it back on the shelf for good. The reader has undertaken this survey of patristic theological currents with the understanding that it is to map out only the principal movements. And so we here rapidly retrace a fifty-year patristic adventure.

---

[11] The Eastern hesitations were by no means provoked exclusively by lofty theological considerations. Politics and personalities played a very important role.

The End of the Affair: Nicaea to Constantinople (325-381)

1. Three years after Nicaea, Emperor Constantine moves well left of center, recalls the Arians from exile, dies an Arian. His Eastern successors remain faithful to his about-face from the Nicene homoousios.

2. *Marcellus of Ancyra* (fl. ca. 325-374), who was on the far right at Nicaea (hence a great champion of the homoousios) goes Sabellian. Here is proof positive that the word homoousios can mean "one in person," and not just theoretically but practically: This is what it did mean for one bishop and his church.

3. These two events provoke an anti-Sabellian alliance in the East—an Eastern surge left-of-center, toward the anti-Nicene, anti-homoousian position we have described.

Until now, there have been no official anti-homoousian conciliar pronouncements in the frightened East. There has been only a telltale silence where the homoousios is concerned, in council after local council and in all their professions of faith; or at best a guarded "We have not lined up behind Arius"—a negative preamble leaving plenty of space for moderate subordinationism, since Arius was a radical. Subordinationism is implied, not expressed. The only position condemned outright in this long series of local or regional councils is Sabellian modalism, the position of the radical right, revealed at Ancyra and suspected elsewhere. But there is a silent, tight-lipped surge of the whole East toward left-of-center, provoked by fear of the word homoousios and of the Western Sabellianism that had just dared raise its head in the East.

4. The East is backing away from the right. This provides a little clique on the radical *left* with its chance to break away and declare the Son simply "unlike the Father"! This is raw subordinationism. These men are more Arian than Arius himself.

5. Thus treacherously attacked from behind by a brand-new radical left while battling toe to toe with the radical right at Ancyra, the East stops retreating from the right. She cuts

short her great slow surge towards a clearer and clearer subordinationism. But what *positive* action is the East to take?

A. Some espoused a "homo*i*ousios"—
   "like in substance" to the Father.
   Utterly like him in all things.

B. Others cried that the "homo*i*ousios"
   was only an iota's distance (the letter *i*)
   from the detested Nicene homoousios. They
   preferred "homoios," simply. "Like" the
   Father somehow. Deliberately vague.

Regrettably, the emperor supports Branch B, and promising Branch A, with its virtually orthodox right wing, is crushed.

Once again we can range the principal theological positions diagrammatically:

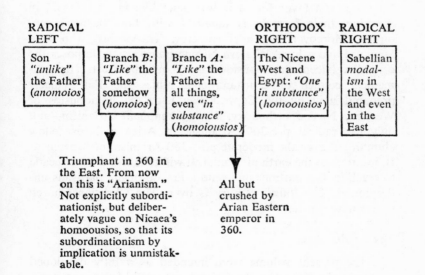

RADICAL LEFT

Son "*unlike*" the Father (*anomoios*)	Branch *B:* "*Like*" the Father somehow (*homoios*)

Branch *A:* "*Like*" the Father in all things, even "*in substance*" (*homoiousios*)

ORTHODOX RIGHT

The Nicene West and Egypt: "*One in substance*" (*homoousios*)

RADICAL RIGHT

Sabellian *modalism* in the West and even in the East

Triumphant in 360 in the East. From now on this is "Arianism." Not explicitly subordinationist, but deliberately vague on Nicaea's homoousios, so that its subordinationism by implication is unmistakable.

All but crushed by Arian Eastern emperor in 360.

What happened has been made famous by Jerome's epigrammatic summary: "The whole world groaned to find itself Arian."

6. But from among the "Arians" of Branch B, victorious in the coup of 360, emerge three of the very greatest doctors of all Christian history. By adding to Movement B's vague and Arian formula ("like" the Father) the phrase "in all things," the three great Cappadocians [12] bring Movement B as far right as defunct Movement A. The Cappadocians (Movement B) do not *say* "like in substance" (defunct Movement A). But in saying "like in all things" they silently and quite intentionally *imply* "like in substance." In fact, in the hands of the Cappadocians the formula "like in all things" is moving later (post-360) "Arianism" very close indeed to the orthodox Nicene "identical in substance," the Nicene homoousios.

7. The last "Arian" (Movement B) emperor is killed. The three great Cappadocians, on Movement B's right wing, are that much freer to propagandize other "Arians" all over the East and win favor for their formula, "like in all things." In *meaning*, their formula is identical with the Nicene homoousios. Moreover, the new emperor, Theodosius, who is a Spaniard and a loyal Western Nicene homoousian, imposes the orthodox Nicene homoousios throughout the East. His ecumenical council of Constantinople rallies the East (nicely prepared now by the Cappadocians) to the homoousios of Western, Nicene orthodoxy. Long-triumphant Arianism—not only the radical pre-360 Arianism of Arius and his fellow alumni, but even the moderate post-360 Arianism of Movement B, is struck to the earth moribund. It will take less than a decade to crush its last bastions and send a few do-or-die partisans underground. The fourth century is over. The Christian Church is again at peace.

The Golden Age

If the present volume were intended as a fully developed history of the fathers of the Church, we would have long pages now on the seven most venerated patristic doctors of the Eastern and Western Churches.[13] The epoch of these seven

[12] See section immediately below, "The Golden Age."
[13] Basil the Great, Gregory of Nazianzus, Gregory of Nyssa, John Chrysostom, Ambrose, Jerome and Augustine.

contemporaries (roughly 350 to 400) is justly honored as the golden age of patristic thought. The only really towering fourth-century figure before mid-century is Athanasius.

But these long pages we shall not have.[14] This is not a history of the fathers of the Church; it is a survey of some of the currents of thought embodied in the fathers of the Church. The fathers of the golden age (except Augustine) are not so much initiators of currents as continuators of currents initiated. Their genius is not so much in their originality as in their orthodoxy. They are not so much wellsprings of thought-currents as watchdogs of Nicaea. Their genius is brought completely into the service of their vocation as pastors of their flocks and guardians of orthodoxy. They do not initiate trends of thought; they channel them.

Once we have examined a current of thought in its origin and early development, we have achieved the purpose of this introductory volume. The best possible understanding of these currents awaits the reader in the very texts of the fathers of the Church—and above all the seven fathers of the golden age— in the other booklets of this series. This is why we are about to consider some features of the golden age fathers in a space altogether incommensurate with their importance for orthodoxy, therefore incommensurate with their importance for us as Christians. May the reader pay far more attention to these fathers in their writings, than we do here in our brief survey.

The three great Cappadocians are Basil the Great, his friend Gregory of Nazianzus, and his brother Gregory of Nyssa. Cappadocia is in Christian "Asia" (modern-day Turkey), which remains the fertile soil for the gospel which it was in the early decades of Christianity. The Cappadocians constitute the classic type of "father of the Church." It was these bishops who finally succeeded in narrowing the technical theological meaning of *ousia* ("being") to "substance," thus rendering the Nicene homoousios unquestionably orthodox in the eyes of the East, so that the East could conscientiously subscribe to it when

[14] Except for Augustine, in our next chapter. His work is mostly early fifth century. Greatest of all the Western fathers, he is a true initiator of currents of thought.

it was reproposed to her at Constantinople I. The latter-day "Arians" (Movement B on page 69), that is, practically the whole of the Christian East, had been mostly terrified anti-Sabellians, to whom the homoousios looked Sabellian [15] before the advent of the Cappadocians. A second means to the same end, the propagation by the same three Cappadocians of an orthodox "Arianism," we have already examined above. Still another important contribution lay in the area of their theology of the processions of the Son and the Holy Spirit.

Basil the Great (fl. 359-379): He was the great administrator among the great Cappadocians. He was the leader of the ex-subordinationist right wing ex-Arians,[16] in which capacity he managed to add "in all things" to the Arian "like the Father," and then pre-negotiated with Athanasius and Pope Damasus the rapprochement of Antioch (379), which Constantinople I confirmed two years later. He wrote for his monastic community the rule which was to become, as "the Rule of St. Basil," the classic model for monastic rules, directing the monastic mentality definitively away from the eremetical ideal toward life in common.[17]

[15] We have discussed at some length the post-Nicene anti-homoousian fears earlier in this chapter.

[16] See above, "Nicaea to Constantinople."

[17] The mention of Basil's monasticism evokes some considerations on monastic literature other than Basil's rule, and on the monastic current in general.

Christian monasticism is by and large a product of the fourth century. The early Christian heroes of grace had been the martyrs. But since the dawn of the century, large-scale martyrdom was a thing of the past, because organized persecution was a thing of the past. Fourth-century Christians suddenly found themselves occupying the coziest, most luxurious places in Roman civilization, now that Christianity was the religion of the empire. For the first time in history it was easy to be a tepid Christian; this provoked a reaction in the fervent. It was monasticism to which they rallied. Monasticism replaced martyrdom as the supreme grace. The new challenge to great souls was no longer the "red martyrdom" but the "white": The new task of the Church's heroes of dedication was no longer to vanquish the enemies of God with their blood, but to vanquish the softness of the Roman Christian world by flight to the desert of solitude, mortification, and contemplation.

Though she was consistently opposed to a martyr-mentality (like that of the Montanists) where there was no real persecution, the Christian Church did, on the other hand, encourage a certain extremism where the evan-

Gregory of Nazianzus (fl. 368-390), the second of the great Cappadocians, is surnamed "the Theologian" because of the eloquent style of his doctrinal discourses. Delicate and restless, perhaps not perfectly stable psychologically, he was able to cope only briefly with the monastic life under his close friend Basil the Great, and later was helpless to keep his hold on the turbulent see of Constantinople. But he was a master of the Greek tongue and literature, a powerful preacher of orthodoxy, and a leader in the anti-Apollinarian polemic.[18]

Gregory of Nyssa (fl. ca. 379-394) was the young brother of Basil and the third of the great Cappadocians. He was perhaps the deepest and tenderest spirit of the patristic Church. An heir of the thought of Origen, he was the one genuinely original and speculative philosopher among the golden age fathers in the East. He was a mystic, and like the other Gregory, a hard-hitting adversary of the Apollinarians. Like

---

gelical counsels were concerned. She gave birth to the monk, that sage reactionary of the desert called by providence to be a new Isaiah, or a new John the Baptist, whose voice crying in the wilderness was to warn Christianity of the menace of death by tepidity. For tepidity can only lead to gradual cooling and eventual freezing. Day in, day out, the monk called his Church to the wilderness: not by insisting that she come bodily in all her members, but calling her there in spirit by the testimony of his own presence in body and soul. He represented her, counterbalancing in the desert the luxury of the cities. And incidentally he attracted streams of pilgrims.

Some of the most influential literature of the patristic age is the direct or indirect product of this new phenomenon. Nearly all of the fathers of the golden age passed a period of their lives as monks. Athanasius' *Life of Antony*, the father of monks, is perhaps the most noteworthy single piece of writing inspired by monasticism. Its force and compelling attraction is attested by Saint Augustine in the *Confessions*. Other examples can be found in the *Conferences* of the great "abbots," in lists of short, pithy, edifying "sayings," and in the desert pilgrims' written accounts of the marvels they witnessed while sojourning with the desert saints.

For two centuries monasticism is to be strictly an Eastern phenomenon. When found in the West (and it is found early and often—Athanasius propagandized it as far north and west as Trier, near today's Luxembourg, during his very first exile, to be followed by Ambrose, Jerome, and Augustine in other lands), it is found as an Eastern export. A good two hundred years separate Antony the Hermit from Benedict of Nursia, whose rule was to be for beginners only, and who would send his "proficient" (spiritually advanced men and women) back to the Rule of Basil.

[18] For Apollinarianism, see chapter 5.

the other Gregory, too, he reproached the Arians for calling upon the man in the street to join in the dispute over delicate theological problems. You ask the money-changer today's rate on some currency, Gregory writes, and you get a dissertation on "begotten" and "unbegotten." You drop into the bakery, and the man behind the counter tells you the Father is greater than the Son. At the baths you ask whether the water is ready, and you are informed that the Son was brought forth from non-existence.[19] (Arius himself had begun it all with dogma in popular songs and doctrine in doggerel.)

John Chrysostom (fl. ca. 385-407) is the ideal preacher of all time, whose eloquent sermons resounded at Antioch for 12 years. After his death he became one of the most widely published and admired of all patristic writers. He headed the difficult see of Constantinople only briefly; half a decade of heated battles ended in his deposition. Chrysostom was a careful, balanced theologian, whose thought was free of tendentiousness.

Currents of thought tend to be one-sided at their source. They are initiated to drive home a point, and are usually the brainchild of some overwhelming insight, or the product of some very great danger for the Church. Consider the apologetes. Consider Origen. Consider Athanasius. But by the year 350 the great patristic currents had already been initiated. The work of balance and synthesis could be undertaken. The great pioneers of this dogmatic balance were the fathers of the golden age, especially Chrysostom, who, if even less original, was even more theologically balanced than the other fathers of the golden age.

Ambrose of Milan (fl. 374-397) was the administrator par excellence, an imperious hierarch whose influence extended not only throughout northern Italy, but into Gaul and even into eastern Europe. It was Ambrose who imposed a public penance on that independent autocrat, Theodosius the Great. He was active in reducing the last Arian bastions after Constantinople I.

[19] Migne, *Patrologia graeca*, volume 46, column 557B. Cited in Marrou, p. 309; cf. Eng. tr., p. 266.

Ambrose had come on the scene as a civil official charged with quelling the riots occasioned by the vacancy of the see of Milan. He brought the disorderly so firmly and impressively in line that the populace by acclamation called him directly from the catecumenate to the episcopacy. Alone of our seven golden age fathers, he was never a monk; yet he saw to it that monasticism in the Eastern style flourished around him at Milan. He is one of the four *egregii doctores* ("great doctors"), with Jerome, Augustine and Gregory the Great, of the Latin Church.

Jerome (fl. 382-419) was author of the Latin Vulgate, today still the official bible of the Latin Church. A fiery and very human scholar, he could be found now fighting with the pope, now translating the scriptures for him. Fresh from a three-year retreat in the desert near Antioch, he organized a monastic movement at Rome, provoked Roman wrath against the innovation, and fled back to the East with his women disciples, who were pioneers among Western nuns. He ended his days as a monk at Bethlehem. Alone among our seven golden age fathers, Jerome was not in episcopal orders.

We borrow again from an outstanding contemporary historian of the ancient Church. Marrou has pointed out typical features in the fathers of the golden age,[20] which we in turn epitomize as follows:

With one exception or so in each case, our seven fathers of the golden age: (1) were born and raised Christian, unlike their predecessors in centuries past; (2) came from the highest echelons of Roman society; (3) received the education expected in gentlemen of leisure; (4) were critically influenced for the better by a mother or sister; (5) began a secular career, usually as a teacher; (6) were "converted" around the age of 30; (7) undertook the monastic life; (8) forsook the monastic life to serve the Church in episcopal sees; (9) were great religious thinkers whose "writings" (more often oral at

---

[20] Marrou, pp. 343-348; cf. Eng. tr., pp. 302-307. The professional historian will already have recognized that in our chapter 4 we are indebted even more than usual to the excellent volume cited in our introduction.

first in an age of sermons and orations), charged with dogma
and biblical commentary, are usually titled "Against . . ."
someone. For our own part we add a characteristic referred
to before: The golden age fathers are (10) much more pastoral guardians of Nicene orthodoxy than initiators of Christian
thought.

In summing up, we can cite Marrou:

> The fathers of the fourth and the beginning of the fifth
> century represent a moment of particularly precious equi-
> librium between, on the one hand, an ancient heritage,
> still relatively untouched by decadence and perfectly as-
> similated, and, on the other hand, a Christian inspiration
> itself arrived at full maturity.[21]

The initiators of patristic currents are past now, and the
ancient heritage they created is the glory of the golden age.
The relative decadence of the later patristic centuries, the
epoch of eclectics and compilers who only regrouped (sometimes grotesquely) elements of the ancient heritage which
pleased each personally, has not yet arrived. This leaves the
fathers of the golden age happily just in the middle, right at
the summit of Christian patristic thought. Current-originating
preoccupations had narrowed their predecessors, and lack of
inspiration (or perhaps surfeit of sources to draw on) would
banalize their successors; but the golden age fathers are too
late to be narrow and too early to be spoiled. Patristic thought
has attained its zenith. Christian theology is in the full flower
of a youthful and vigorous maturity.

QUESTIONS FOR DISCUSSION

1. Which century is the greatest of patristic centuries? Can
   you name a half-dozen giants of Christian thought from
   that century?
2. Describe the error of Arius of Alexandria. What truth
   does he begin with, only to end in error?
3. What did Arius do when driven from Alexandria?

[21] Marrou, p. 343; cf. Eng. tr., p. 304.

4. What did Emperor Constantine undertake in order to halt the furor?

5. Describe the rather "open fan" of diverse theological tendencies that came to light at Nicaea.

6. What is "homogeneous evolution of dogma"?

7. Were the Christian Roman emperors representative of "caesaropapism"? Explain.

8. Identify the great champion of Nicaea, and sketch his theological tack against the Arians.

9. Why did the bishops of the East, apparently happy to proclaim the homoousios at Nicaea, shortly withdraw their signatures?

10. Sketch "the twisting trail from Nicaea I to Constantinople I," the history of an Arianism condemned but not crushed. Emphasize the year 360 as a turning point.

11. Identify: Basil the Great, Gregory of Nazianzus, Gregory of Nyssa, John Chrysostom, Ambrose, and Jerome. Why do they get such brief treatment in this booklet?

12. What occasioned the rise of monasticism? What was the function of the monk in the Church? How did monasticism come from East to West?

13. Describe the ideal type of "father of the Church," the typical father of the golden age.

14. What did the fathers of A.D. 100-350 sow that the golden-age fathers (350-430) reaped? What did the earlier fathers lack that the golden-age fathers supplied? Why are the later fathers (430-750) to be considered generally inferior to the golden-age fathers?

FURTHER PROBLEMS

1. After a preliminary clarification of the distinction between homogeneous and non-homogeneous evolution of dogma, show how twentieth-century dogma is homogeneous with that of the patristic Church, or with the teachings of the bible.

Let someone play the devil's advocate, attempting to demonstrate a non-homogeneous evolution of new doctrine not to be found in scripture and early Church tradition: for example, not to be found before the first ecumenical council.

One might discuss:

    a. Christ, one divine Person in two natures, divine and human. (Compare discussion problem 3 following chapter 5.)

    b. One or another of the sacraments. The "Real Presence."

    c. Three really distinct, but inseparable, divine Persons in one God (in one sole divine nature).

    d. Papal infallibility and universal jurisdiction. (Compare discussion problem 2 following chapter 2.)

2. After a preliminary recapitulation of the function of the monk in the Church at monasticism's birth in the fourth century, discuss the function of the monk in the Church of the twentieth century. Where do "religious" who are neither monks nor secular priests fit in? (There were no religious of this intermediate type, at least not organized into "orders" or "congregations" in our modern sense, in the early Church.)

Chapter 5: The Fifth Century

GRACE IN THE WEST:
THE CHRISTOLOGICAL ADVENTURE
IN THE EAST

Augustine

The last of the golden-age fathers and perhaps the greatest
—unquestionably the greatest father of the Western Church—
must receive more than a passing notice. In a study of the
currents of early Christian thought, *Augustine* has many times
the stature of any of the other six, for Augustine originated
currents of thought, while the other six merely enriched them
and passed them on. It is partly because of his towering personal genius—but it is also partly because this genius is pure
Latin in a Christendom whose theology has been almost all
Greek, and partly because more than any other of our seven
golden-age fathers he is self-educated, and partly because of
new, purely Western heresies assailing his African homeland
—that Augustine, Bishop of Hippo, is an original thinker who
had no peer among his Eastern contemporaries. The latter
had been all caught up with the single, old, theologically defeated Arian heresy. They had had to strike out at it again
and again before it would die in the hearts of its fanatics.
Then, when that struggle was over, the East was at peace and
her theologians were busy consolidating. But Augustine had
only begun his battles.

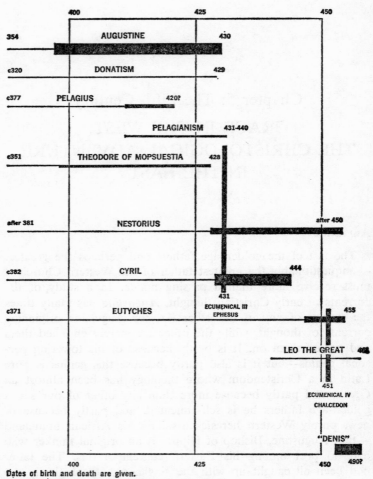

	400	425	450
354	AUGUSTINE	430	
c320	DONATISM	429	
c377	PELAGIUS	420?	
	PELAGIANISM	431-440	
c351	THEODORE OF MOPSUESTIA	428	
after 381	NESTORIUS		after 450
c382	CYRIL	444	
	431	ECUMENICAL III	
c371	EUTYCHES	EPHESUS	455
		LEO THE GREAT	461
		451	
		ECUMENICAL IV	
		CHALCEDON	
		"DENIS"	
	400	425	450	490?

Dates of birth and death are given.
Heavy lines indicate approximately when writer "flourished."

Augustine flourished from about the turn of the century, i.e., between 397-430. What connects the fourth and fifth centuries is therefore the end of the golden age.

The City of God

At the first fall of the "Eternal City" of Rome to barbarian invaders (410), Augustine, across the Mediterranean, meditated the awful thing for scores of long, depressing hours. His faith was shaken. Not his Christian faith, but his Roman faith—that the visible kingdom of Christ on earth might be the Empire. His meditations may have helped make him something of a pessimistic thinker. Pessimism is a trait that allegedly marks his anti-Pelagian polemic. It also allegedly marks Latin theology of grace (up to and including the heterodox "black predestination"—positive reprobation—of modern times) in striking contrast to the Eastern concept of man's full restoration and divinization in Christ. But the authentically Christian pessimism of his insight into the radical instability of the City of This Earth is, on the contrary, in no way to be regretted. The collapse of Rome awakened Augustine to the invisible nature of the City of God, the society of the predestined; and, correspondingly, to the invisible nature of the City of Earth, the community of all those who will find themselves one day in hell.

True, the City of God, the society of those predestined to heaven, is to an important extent commensurate with the visible kingdom of God on earth, the visible Christian Church. And true, the City of Earth, the society whose end will be death and destruction forever in hell, is to an important extent commensurate with the decaying Roman empire, which had just given so striking a token of its ultimate destructibility in the fall of its capital. But the City of God on earth is also invisible: The saints of the Old Testament, as well as pagans of goodwill who had never been suspected of "belonging," are a part of its citizenry, as will come to light in the next life. Thus the City of God extends beyond the visible kingdom of God, the Church, and includes an invisible component outside the Church. Similarly, the City of Earth extends beyond the pagan element of the doomed empire, encroaching even upon the visible Christian Church: There will be Christians in hell. This delicate equilibrium between an invisible-visible City of God, and a visible-invisible City of Earth, all the former on its way to heaven and all the latter on its way to hell, is a concept calculated to identify a great religious genius, and alone would have sufficed to rank Augustine among the Western doctors of the first order.[1] Add his anti-Pelagian [2] polemic (his doctrine of grace and free will) and his *De Trinitate* (the first genuinely Western theology of the Trinity, according to Marrou)—even neglecting his other polemics and the enormous catalog of his pastoral and spiritual compositions—and he becomes ever so easily the greatest of the Latin fathers.

The Donatist Schism

At the dawn of the preceding century, after the last great persecution (Diocletian's: brief in time [303-305]), but the fiercest of all), a certain Melitius judged the hierarchy too lenient with repentant apostates and went into schism, molding a new little sect of saints, a fiery little church of iron men who had not collapsed under the lash. Athanasius broke them, however, with one stroke of his lash, and if they persisted feebly thereafter it was without consequence for the history of patristic thought.

A few years later (in 312) the Carthaginian *Donatus* went into schism for a like cause—hierarchical leniency toward repentant bishops who had handed over the sacred books

[1] This equilibrium between the visible and invisible aspects of the Cities of God and Satan, delicate balance though it be, is so abundantly clear, woven and interwoven into every book of *The City of God* that it is puzzling to read certain modern scholars who have taken Augustine's City of God to be the visible Church and his City of Earth to be the Roman empire: Church and State. This naiveté is all the more astonishing in view of the fact that *The City of God* is the foremost work of the foremost Latin father, and one of the most widely read masterpieces in all literature.

[2] See below, "The Great Onslaught: Pelagius."

to the imperial gestapo in the same persecution of 303. This time the results were much more serious than in the Melitian schism, and Augustine a century later had a major polemic on his hands. In the twinkling of an eye half of the hundred sees around Carthage were Christian and half of them Donatist, many with two bishops each. The Donatists declared invalid the sacraments (1) administered by the bishops who had handed over the sacred books, however repentant now—or (2) administered by any of their successors, however innocent personally—or (3) administered by any bishop who refused to excommunicate either category—or (4) administered by any of the successors of these last. In other words, the Donatists stood against the whole Catholic Church in Africa. Catholics who came to Donatism were rebaptized.

Despite a long police-state persecution the Donatists waxed and persevered for over a hundred years. They threw themselves in the path of their persecutors, winning a "martyrdom" like the martyrdom of their fathers under Diocletian. There were cases of mass suicides. Only the Vandal cataclysm of 429 put an end to the Donatists.

In reaction to the Donatist schism the Latin Church further clarified the doctrine of the validity of sacraments administered by unworthy ministers, and also clarified her ecclesiology of a truly catholic, universal Church, with which one must be in communion in order to share full membership in the living body of Christ—personal fervor does not suffice.

The Great Onslaught: Pelagius

No sooner had Augustine's already practiced pen dealt the Donatists their heaviest theological blow (411-413—Augustine was the surprising new star of a Carthaginian council) when more trouble arrived in Africa, this time in the person of *Pelagius* (fl. ca. 411-420), a British monk fleeing fallen Rome. Pelagius' name had preceded him: he was a fine ascetic but a poor theologian. Augustine resharpened his quill. But Pelagius tarried in Africa only long enough to indoctrinate a certain Celestius, then moved on to the East. So it was the hapless Celestius who first felt the sting of that masterful quill, already notched with the defeats of Donatists and Manichaeans and now black with the ink of the amplest inkwell in the history of Christian polemic.

Pelagius, like Arius, held a single-truth theory. Pelagius' point of departure was perfectly orthodox, only it was one-sided: Man owes God obedience, and is capable of rendering it. But Pelagius, like Arius, was insensible to the delicacy of the truth he was preparing to handle so carelessly, the truth he was preparing to oversimplify. Pelagius had not meditated and assimilated the Christian paradox: Man cannot serve God unless God gives him the power to do it, and yet when man does not serve God man alone is at fault. To Pelagius, just as, much later, to certain extremists among the Calvinists, this delicately balanced two-sided truth looked not so much like a mystery as like a choice. Pelagius opted for man's responsibility and downgraded God's grace. Instead of being a theologian, Pelagius was an untheological (i.e., man-centered) moralist: He eliminated original sin, then made every actual sin mortal. (Christ? Marvelous example to follow. But a genuinely redemptive cross and resurrection are out of the question.)

Very briefly, Pelagius held that man can live a sinless life and save his soul without grace.

Whereupon Augustine—God-centered to begin with—laid so much stress on God's grace that he underplayed in his polemic the role of free will. One day extreme Calvinists, and Jansenists, would claim him as their doctor par excellence. And indeed in his anti-Pelagian polemic Augustine does lay heavy stress on predestination.

To speak merely of Augustine's "anti-Pelagian polemic" may not be strong enough. Perhaps we should be willing to see in Augustine, as that long, tiresome polemic wore on and on, a kind of a personal pessimism about sin and predestination, nesting conveniently in the same branch of his psychology as his pessimism about the doomed, sinful City of Earth. Perhaps. But it is pure nonsense to allege that predestination is all Augustine taught. One has only to look at his earlier treatise *On Free Choice*. Pelagius himself taunts Augustine with what he has written there in powerful exaltation of God's supreme natural gift to man (Pelagius was to call it God's only "grace"), free will. No, we can with certainty reproach Augustine only for allowing the exigencies of the Pelagian polemic to draw him into a one-sided consideration of the mystery of grace and free will. Once Pelagius had divided the mystery into halves in order to discard grace, Augustine proceeded to divide it into halves (conceptually) in order to save grace. So far, all is in good order. A separate consideration of the activity of grace and the activity of free will is legitimate, since grace and free will are not identical. However, in order to save grace, Augustine, in the Pelagian polemic, underplayed free will. Augustine allowed Pelagius to choose his own battlefield, an artificially engineered terrain whose advantages were all on the side of Pelagius. No wonder it took gallons of ink to defeat him. A lesser man than Augustine would easily have lost to Pelagius. Grace and free will now suddenly appear as two spiritual cogs that somehow have to be made to mesh in spite of their incommensurability, instead of as two facets of one single mystery.

In other words, Pelagius severed the Christian mystery that it is God who determines us (by grace) to choose this or that (freely).[3] Pelagius rejects grace. Whereupon Augustine undertakes to "reconcile grace and free will," as we like to say. This he does by stressing grace (which he should do) to the extent that he seems to undervalue free will (which of course he should not do).

But in yielding to Pelagius' division of the mystery, Augustine did not fall into what the history of heresy shows to be the almost inevitable consequence of dividing mysteries in two: He did not make a choice between the two halves. He attempted to balance them. If he overconceptualized the

---

[3] Augustine's words earlier in his career, in his treatise *On Free Choice*.

mystery and tried to explain too much of it, at least he did not contort it. For this alone he is a blessed prodigy in the history of Christian thought.[4]

After a full decade of polemics, conciliar and papal condemnations, and the zeal of the imperial police, Pelagius killed himself and his heresy died with him, except for pockets of resistance in Italy and Britain. Driven from Italy, the heresy fled east to the shelter of Nestorius. This was very poor timing. Two years later the Council of Ephesus solemnly condemned Pelagianism along with, and because of, its new patron. At about the same time Pelagianism was wiped out in Britain (whence Pelagius had originally come) by a missionary task force. A last uprising, once more in Italy, met a quick end a decade after Augustine's death, and from that time forward Pelagianism was only a fanatical underground, having little direct impact on Christian thought.[5] Its proponents took to signing their writings with orthodox pseudonyms. A host of names were used—including the name of Augustine of Hippo!

We return to the East for the remainder of the chapter, to a territory forever untroubled by quarrels on grace and free will.

---

[4] Ultimately because of Augustine, Bañez and Molina will renew the struggle to "explain grace and free will" a thousand years later, with anything but complete success, and their struggle will continue down to our own century.

[5] But its spirit never completely died. Pelagius is the patron saint of Western voluntarism. Have we never heard that still, small voice, common property of most of us Christians west of the Adriatic, whispering somewhere inside us that we can resist this temptation or perform this good work if only we *will* to, if only we exert ourselves? This is the truth, of course. But the voice neglects to add that we cannot if *God* "will" not. It is the ghost of old Pelagius, kept half-alive by the spirit of businessman's piety, the spirit of enterprise, of self-reliance, of mistrust of exaggerated mysticism, the spirit of many a good occidental drive which becomes dangerous when carried too far.

Of course, God "will" if we ask him to. (Or even if we do not, we always have the grace to resist temptation.) But then again we cannot even ask him to unless he first moves us to ask him to! (The heresy that denies this is one day to be called "semi-Pelagianism.") Practical solution: We ask him to, and thank him for the very prayer he is making possible and actual in us.

The Apollinarian Heresy

The Greek battlefield of the fourth century had been trinitarian. Now it was to be Christological. Is Christ one person or two? Has he one nature or two?

Has Christ a human soul? A certain Apollinarius had said no (still in Arian times). Healthy trinitarian rightist that he was (a Nicene homoousian), indeed Athanasius' bulwark in Arian Syria, it is curious that Apollinarius was so "Arian" when it came to Christology. The Arians of the radical left (if not the first Arians, then at least the radicals of the later desperate leftward plunge) [6] had said no: Christ's human body has the Son, the Word, for a soul. This premise enabled them to argue the inferiority of the Word from the facts of the gospel—from Jesus' hunger, thirst, fatigue, and tears. No soul that suffered such things could be consubstantial (homoousios) with the Father. This was quite "unlike (*an-omoios*) the Father." Undoubtedly his outlook was colored by the fact that around him in Syria practically everyone was Arian,[7] anti-homoousian.[8] Whatever the reason be, Apollinarius taught that in Christ the divine Word, consubstantial with the Father, supplied the functions of the human soul. The Word had taken flesh without taking on a human spirit.

Apollinarius' reason for depriving Christ of a human soul was to withdraw him all the more surely from sin. But the road to heresy is paved with good intentions. Towards the end of his life Apollinarius was condemned by a multitude of local and regional councils, by the emperor (whose police force included a crack heresy-squad) and most effectively of all by the three great Cappadocians.[9]

[6] See our chart, page 69, in chapter 4.

[7] Neo-Arian, "Movement B" of our chart in chapter 4.

[8] We might summarize and contrast Arianism and Apollinarianism this way: Arianism saw Christ as union of a half-God and a half-man; Apollinarius saw Christ as union of perfect God and a half-man.

[9] See chapter 4, above.

The Nestorian Heresy

Why have we gone back into the fourth century, to Apollinarianism, in our history of the fifth century? Or rather, why have we kept fourth-century Apollinarianism until now? Because indirectly Apollinarius set the stage for *Nestorius* (fl. ca. 428-451).

Apollinarius had so disgusted a certain Diodore of Tarsus (we are still momentarily in the fourth century) that the latter went to the other extreme. Christ, said Diodore, not only had a whole human nature, including a human soul; but this human nature was so complete that the Son of God is to be distinguished from the son of Mary. "Only one Son, of course," added Diodore lamely, forgetting that a son is necessarily *someone,* so that in distinguishing two sons, he really destroyed Christ's unity. Diodore erred, in the opposite direction from Appollinarius. He had come within a hair's breadth of attributing to Christ what we today call a human *person.*

The third and final prelude to the *pièce de résistance* was played by *Theodore of Mopsuestia* (fl. 398-428). (At last we have reached the dawn of our fifth century.) A faithful disciple of Diodore, Theodore taught that there were two sons (and two lords). To explain their union, Theodore employed the Greek word *sunapheia,* "clinging together," a strong word reminiscent of the marriage act, the closest natural created union of two persons, who while "becoming each other" in flesh, will, emotions, intellect, interests, sympathies, "soul"— *almost* their whole being—remain nonetheless two persons. We may be here in the presence of a marvelously apt analogy for the union of Christ's godhood and manhood. But it is only an analogy. Theodore's attempt to define and name the union of Christ's natures as a *sunapheia* is to fall short of the reality. Theodore had erred, in the same direction as Diodore.[10]

[10] He never knew it—his condemnation came more than a century after his demise, at Chalcedon (see below). Today some scholars are inclined to say that he had done quite well, considering what a truly "ineffable" (to use his own word) union he had undertaken to name, and considering that Nestorius had not yet prolonged his current of thought into open heresy.

The pendulum was swinging wildly. Apollinarius: no human soul. Diodore and Theodore: a complete human son. Both extremes are erroneous. Will there now arise some powerful orthodox theologian to take the situation in hand, balance out the extremes, explicitate the Christian doctrine of one divine Person in two complete natures and bring the pendulum to rest at its orthodox midpoint?

There was as yet no one to bring it to rest. It broke free in the anti-Apollinarian direction of Diodore and Theodore.

Nestorius, a direct, uncompromising, violent personage, installed in the mighty episcopal chair of Constantinople, suddenly threw all his great weight in the direction mapped out by Diodore and Theodore. Did God die on the cross? Is Mary God's mother? No, Nestorius implies, only creatures can die or be born, not God.

Now came the reaction, at Constantinople itself, at Rome, and especially at Alexandria. It was instantaneous and unfavorable.

Nemesis of Nestorius: Cyril of Alexandria

The metropolitan of Egypt, *Cyril* (fl. 429-444), was by nature passionate. Fire was going to be used to fight fire. The proud and tough Nestorius had so drastically distinguished the Son of God from the son of Mary that Christ was implicitly asserted to have what we call today two persons.[11] Cyril of Alexandria took the offensive. Taking the central salvific fact of the divinity of Christ ("If Christ is God . . .") he welded it to his own central intuition of the concrete unity of Christ's being ("If Christ is God and Mary is his mother . . .") and forged a doctrine of a genuine incarnation of God (". . . then how is she not God's mother?"). Cyril termed this concrete unity of Christ's being the "hypostatic union." Today, when we want to express concrete unity of being we often say simply "unity of person," but we have retained the Cyrillian "hypostatic union" as a synonym.

[11] Like Diodore, however, he explicitly rejected the notion of the "two sons."

Cyril also saw fit to appropriate the phrase,[12] "One nature, incarnate, of the Word of God." It was perfectly capable of expressing the concept of the incarnation. It succeeded where Theodore's weak "clinging together" had failed: It straightforwardly said *one*. No question of mere clinging. Today the formula would be heretical (monophysite), because today "nature" means essence or substance, of which Christ of course has two, divine and human, not one. But in the early fifth century "nature" (*"physis"*) was capable of denoting that concrete unity of being which today we call "person." Thus in the early fifth century Cyril's phrase was perfectly orthodox: "One nature (i.e., concrete unity of being), incarnate, of the Word of God." Today a Christian would say, "One person, incarnate, of the Word of God."

"One nature, incarnate, of the Word of God": a gem of an epitome—in the sense in which it was meant. But Cyril's gem would cost him dearly, posthumously. (Unfortunately, "nature" could also mean, even in the fifth century, what it means today! But we must not get ahead of our story.)

In the meantime it is Nestorius who is going to pay, and not posthumously. Cyril besieged in writing everyone whose influence could weigh in the balance—the emperor, the empress, princesses, and the pope. Most helpful of all in this instance was the pope. He demanded of Nestorius a retraction. Unfortunately however, he specified that the retraction be made through Cyril.

Not content to have the patriarch of Constantinople on his knees, this patriarch of Alexandria wanted him to grovel in the dust. Cyril went beyond his papal mandate and demanded of Nestorius not just the retractation, but a positive profession of the opposite theology of Christ's unity, in Cyril's own, carefully chosen words, including his especially embarrassing "Twelve Anathematisms." The formularies laid on the table for Nestorius' signature were Cyril's personally; they were (for the times) ambiguous (e.g., "Anathema to him who does

---

[12] Not knowing that it was first used, in a less orthodox way, by Apollinarius! Cf. Marrou, p. 381; in Eng. tr., p. 344.

not confess that the Word has suffered in the flesh"), and (at the time) nothing like defined dogma.

Nestorius of course refused. In the explosion that ensued the emperor convoked an ecumenical council.

The Third Ecumenical Council: Ephesus (431)

Nestorius had played with fire. He had called into question the divine motherhood of the Virgin Mary. As in the days of Arius, Everyman was a street-corner theologian and, as in all ages since, Catholics have reacted violently when Mary was attacked in any way. The very streets which five centuries before had resounded about the ears of a hapless Paul with the cry, "Great is Diana of the Ephesians!" now rang, we are told, with the name of Mary as Mother of God. It did not take the grave fathers indoors long to ratify the definition of the less grave citizenry in the streets—especially as Cyril, characteristically, had the decision against Nestorius ratified before the arrival of the opposing party. Nestorius suddenly found himself deposed.

The bishops of Antioch and Syria were supposed to have been the party supporting Nestorius. Antioch, in recent years [13] consistently Alexandria's contrary theological pole and rival patriarchate, was deeply suspicious of Cyril's formula. Antioch had good reason to be. Ambiguous in formulation and unilateral in promulgation, however orthodox in content, the theology of Cyril of Alexandria merited a little probing. Cyril had not had the catholicity to consult his neighbor patriarchate on the formulation of Christian dogma when he undertook to condemn Nestorius. Who, then, was to say it was Christian dogma? One single patriarchate? Incensed, John of Antioch "deposed" Cyril of Alexandria. Whereupon Cyril naturally "deposed" John. (The emperor promptly deposed and imprisoned both. Then he restored them both, and exiled Nestorius.)

At last the true personal greatness of two genuinely great men came to the surface. Cyril and John negotiated. They

[13] Except in the matter of biblical interpretation, where Antioch's scientific and literal exegesis had contrasted with Alexandrian allegorism for a century.

negotiated long and hard and honestly—and they succeeded. John accepted the *fait accompli* of Cyril's unilateral deposition of Nestorius at Ephesus, and Cyril accepted a new Antiochene Christological creed which even dared correct one of his proud anathematisms.

The Syrian formula was indeed one calculated to please both sides of the quarrel. Its content and expression was really no more Antiochene (in emphasizing the distinction of Christ's natures) than it was Alexandrian (in emphasizing the concrete unity of Christ's being, his "Person"). Its key formula is a veritable marvel of Christological balance: [14] Christ's two natures enjoy a "union without mixture." (Today we specify, unity of *person* without mixture of natures.)

Nestorius had exaggerated the Antiochene "without mixture," so that he implicitly had, as a result, two persons along with the two natures. In the near future new heretics would exaggerate the personal union of the natures so as to force the human nature into the divine. But union without mixture is the delicate balance required by orthodoxy, and we owe it to old enemies cooperating. Each had had half the truth: "Consubstantial with his Father in his divinity, consubstantial with us in his humanity," says the compromise creed. They found that the whole truth had been shared between them all along.[15]

The Monophysitism of Eutyches

Nestorius had exaggerated the natures "without mixture" into natures separated, so that each nature implicitly entailed a corresponding person. Now *Eutyches* (fl. ca. 445-455), influential superior of hundreds of monks and influential friend of the imperial court at Constantinople (Nestorius' see!), propagated the contrary and symmetrical exaggeration. The union of Christ's natures, the concrete unity of being in God

[14] It reproduces in essence a formula which had been the property of the Nestorian faction. Not all the "Nestorians" were as Nestorian as our modern summaries of Nestorianism might suggest.

[15] Nestorianism never died, despite the patriarchs' ultimate accord on its condemnation. See chapter 6.

incarnate, the "unity of person" (we say), the "hypostatic union" (Cyril had said) becomes in Eutyches not a personal unity of unmixed natures but a mixture of the natures. The finite nature is swallowed up in the infinite, so that Christ's sole nature is the divine nature. He is God, but he is not man. Christ indeed is "from" two natures, holds Eutyches—but when the two natures, God's and man's, met in the incarnation, the only nature to survive the ineffable encounter was God's.

The monophysites had ready-made support in Cyril's ingenious formula: "One nature, incarnate, of the Word of God." They appropriated it as if "nature" meant what it means today: essence or substance. (And well it could in itself, even in the fifth century.) And for good measure they appropriated as sponsor Cyril himself. Having died only a few years earlier, he was in no position to refuse the invitation to become the great doctor of the monophysites.

The Fourth Ecumenical Council: Chalcedon (451)

Condemned at Constantinople, Eutyches used his court influence to schedule a "fourth ecumenical" council (illegitimate!), called "Ephesus II," consisting mostly of peasant monks armed with clubs, who readily "rehabilitated" Eutyches and repudiated the clear, balanced, precise *Tome to Flavian* (composed by *Pope Leo The Great* [fl. 440-461]), a classic of Christological formulary designed to condemn monophysitism without going back to Nestorianism.[16] The case was closed. Eutyches was victor, and Emperor Theodosius II would hear no appeals.

---

[16] The *Tomus* was a letter from Rome, in the mighty person of her chief bishop Leo, to the Patriarch of Constantinople. For these few wondrously well-wrought phrases, soon to become *de fide* at Chalcedon, and for his dogmatic sermons, admirable alike for their content and style, Pope Leo the Great ranks as a father of the Church.

It was Leo himself who gave the abortive Eutychian "Ephesus II" its permanent name in history: the Robber Synod. "It was not a conciliar assembly," wrote Leo, "but a convention of bandits": *Non judicium sed latrocinium.*

Suddenly, unexpectedly, Theodosius was dead. Chalcedon was convoked and the bad deeds of the "Robber Synod," the Eutychian "Ephesus II" were speedily undone: Monophysitism was condemned and Leo's *Tome* was approved, to become the final piece of fifth-century Christological formulary.[17] But monophysitism never died, at least not in name. It became less radical, most likely even orthodox, and is still alive today in the Eastern Christian Church that calls itself "Monophysite."

"Denis the Areopagite"

Late in the fifth century there appears, as if from nowhere, an unknown genius of the first order, a neo-Platonist destined forever to exercise a massive influence on all Greek theology. Following a received custom of the time, he employs as *nom de plume* a name already respected by his audience in order to win a favorable reading, convinced that the reader will have been so thoroughly benefited by the truth of what he has read that he will not really have been deceived in any practical way.

"*Denis the Areopagite*" (fl. ca. 480) succeeded so well, with both pseudonym and presentation of what he saw as the truth, that the whole corps of fathers after him not only reverenced his purloined identity (Paul had a convert named Denis the Areopagite: Acts 17:34) but accepted his strange mystical doctrine as well, even if they often had to purify it of unorthodox elements (the greatest of his disciples would be his orthodox interpreter, Maximus the Confessor).[18]

Like Origen, "Denis" teaches a hierarchical universe, descending from a God who is above all being, and moving

---

[17] The first was Cyril's "One nature, incarnate, of the Word of God" (orthodox while *his* meaning lasted; it was ambiguous). The second was Antioch's "union without mixture . . . consubstantial with his Father in divinity, consubstantial with us in humanity."

[18] Thomas Aquinas is another, and better known, master of the surreptitious rectification of "Denis the Areopagite." St. Thomas deliberately misinterprets "Denis" to make "Denis" orthodox. Thus, in the spirit of the age, St. Thomas uses the respected Areopagite to get an "authority" to witness to what Thomas is teaching.

through the highest spirits uninterruptedly to the lowest material creation. A kind of spiritual light invests these creations, descending from the pure uncreated light of God in successive diminutions at each step down the ladder of creation. Man can ascend to the vision of God in a kind of passive ecstasy. "Denis'" mystical insights are often far more valid than their partially orthodox theoretical justification.

Let us attempt to recapitulate the fifth century.

The West struggled over Christian man, and the question was functional: how grace and free will operate. The victor was Augustine, the vanquished was Pelagius.

The East struggled over Christ, and the question was ontological: the being of Christ. The victors were Cyril of Alexandria, Ephesus, and Chalcedon; the vanquished were Nestorius, and Eutyches the monophysite.

QUESTIONS FOR DISCUSSION

1. What patristic phenomenon links the fourth and fifth centuries?
2. Who is the greatest father of the Western Church? Where did he live? What was his office?
3. Can you account for his greatness and originality?
4. Name, describe, and discuss his masterwork. Is it a treatise on Church and State?
5. Enumerate Augustine's three or four greatest contributions to Western theology.
6. Describe the rise of Donatism. Where did it flourish? How did "evolution of dogma" profit from its errors?
7. Describe Augustine's gigantic anti-Pelagian polemic. Here are possible bases for a step-by-step discussion: a. Who was Pelagius? b. What did he overstress? c. What did Augustine stress in return? d. Where was Augustine nearly trapped and defeated? How did he rescue himself? e. What became of Pelagius and Pelagianism after Augustine's victory?
8. What was Apollinarianism?

9. What were the reactions in the opposite direction? (There was a series of three.)
10. Who defeated Nestorius and what was his central intuition?
11. What is his famous Christological formulary? Why would it have been heretical today, whereas it was orthodox then?
12. Where and by what means did he defeat Nestorius?
13. Why was Antioch anti-Cyrillian?
14. Recount the reconciliation of Antioch and Cyril's Alexandria. How did Antioch's compromise Christological formula fit in?
15. Where and what did Eutyches teach?
16. Whom did the monophysites appropriate as their doctor? How?
17. Who had the "Robber Synod" convoked, and what were its deeds?
18. What was the *Tome to Flavian?*
19. Where and how was the "Robber Synod" undone?
20. When did "Denis the Areopagite" live? What did he teach?
21. Capsulize the fifth century.

FURTHER PROBLEMS

1. When you perform a good action under the influence of grace, do you perform the whole action, or rather only a part so that God or God's grace performs the rest? If only a part, then what part do you perform and what part does God perform? Or do you perform the whole action, while God simultaneously performs the whole action through you? Test your opinion against concrete examples, like resisting a temptation, or speaking a kind word to an unpleasant, ungrateful person. More briefly, do God and the Christian work "fifty-fifty," or does each do everything?
2. Do you think that the Christians you know tend unconsciously to be Apollinarians? Were you an Apollinarian in grade school or high school? Jesus never sinned, because

he is God. But do you think he ever worried? Did he ever "wonder about" things? Did he learn from his mother things he had never known? Did he really feel abandoned on the cross, feel less hope than you would feel at the most hopeless moment of your life? Did he ever laugh? Was he *genuinely* taken aback at the "little faith" he encountered after so much careful instruction and so many well-known wonders?

3. Can you take Cyril's expression, "One nature, incarnate, of the Word of God," and find in it all three essentials of ancient and modern orthodox Christology: a. one divine Person (the second Person of the Trinity); b. the divine nature; c. a human nature?

4. "As in the days of Arius," so in the days of Nestorius "Everyman was a street-corner theologian." Why is this no longer true? Should this spirit be recaptured?

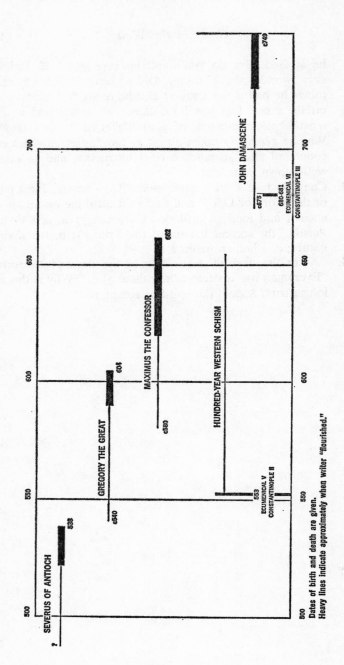

SEVERUS OF ANTIOCH

538

GREGORY THE GREAT

c540

604

MAXIMUS THE CONFESSOR

c580

662

HUNDRED-YEAR WESTERN SCHISM

553
ECUMENICAL V
CONSTANTINOPLE II

JOHN DAMASCENE

c675

c749

680-681
ECUMENICAL VI
CONSTANTINOPLE III

500   550   600   650   700

Dates of birth and death are given.
Heavy lines indicate approximately when writer "flourished."

Chapter 6

The Sixth, Seventh and Eighth Centuries
WANE AND DEMISE

The Indestructibility of "Monophysitism"

The monophysites outlived Eutyches, outlived fourteen centuries of persecution beginning with that of a Roman police-
state, and they live today in the Monophysite Church—a few
hundred thousand in Syria, Palestine, Egypt, and the United
States, several million in Ethiopia and Armenia. They will
never, they say, accept that Nestorian synod of Chalcedon that
Catholics and Orthodox [1] alike call ecumenical and infallible.

We have seen the solidarity of all Egypt with Alexandria.
If Alexandria was orthodox, Egypt was automatically orthodox
(as under the leadership of Athanasius fighting the Arians,
in contrast to almost the whole East). But if Alexandria were
to be monophysite . . .

[1] The ordinary word "orthodox," which we have employed dozens of
times through five chapters, is susceptible, after Chalcedon, of a very
special additional and credal meaning, in which case it is capitalized. It
denotes *the Church* which, unlike the Monophysite Church, accepts
Chalcedon. "Orthodox" and "Catholic" are therefore synonymous—until
sometime after the eighth-century ecumenical council (Nicaea II, 787),
when the patriarchate of the West and the Eastern patriarchates broke
off communion; they remain in a state of schism to this very day. The
patriarchate of the West appropriated the name "Catholic Church," and
the Eastern Churches the name "Orthodox Church" for convenience, for
each claims to be both catholic and orthodox. (Hence they are sometimes
called "Roman Catholic" and "Eastern Orthodox" to distinguish them
more clearly.)

99

A century after the death of Athanasius, Alexandria was monophysite, and Egypt with her.

Alexandria had a special historical reason for being monophysite. Champion of the unity of Christ's person at Ecumenical Council III (Ephesus), she felt rebuffed at the Antiochene victory of Christ's two natures at Ecumenical Council IV (Chalcedon). She had always felt that Antioch distinguished in Christ not just two natures but two persons. How, then, could the Council of Chalcedon, Antioch's triumph, be other than Nestorian? Alexandria, therefore, determined upon an anti-Chalcedonian theology and Egypt went with her. Monophysitism became a kind of Egyptian national religion.

There were wondrous intellectual gymnastics, psychologically naive but logically ineluctable, and they testify to the theological tensions of the monophysite Egyptian Church. She split and resplit on the basis of the contradictory, inescapable consequences of her principle of a single divine nature for the carpenter of Nazareth. What of his body? It was a phantom body. Or, on the contrary, it was not only real, it was eternal and uncreated, because it was God. Or thirdly (a mid-position) it was preserved incorruptible by the Word (which is orthodoxy, of all things). Or even, since Christ's single Person requires a single nature, then the Trinity must have three natures because it has three Persons! Thus the very vitality of Egyptian monophysite theology weakened the Egyptian Church by generating enthusiastic internal schisms along the lines of fantastic currents of thought.

The Armenian Church, too, mostly because it was antihellenistic, was anti-Chalcedon. And it is "monophysite" to this very day.

Once upon a time the land of Ethiopia had been orthodox, thanks to its contact with the great Athanasius himself. Frumentios, a Christian slave of the Ethiopians, who had been captured years before and had grown to manhood among his captors, attained to the incomparably influential position of tutor to the crown prince. Suddenly he appeared at the episcopal palace of Alexandria with the news that there was a vast and ready hearing for the gospel at the bottom of the world. Would his Excellency only see fit to send a mission? Athanasius acceded, discerned in Frumentios himself the best candidate for bishop, consecrated him, and sent him back to evangelize Ethiopia in strict Nicene orthodoxy. But in the post-Chalcedon unrest, Ethiopia fell to a piety and zeal as ardent as that of Frumentios: Ethiopia went monophysite.

Nubia too: Justinian had sent an orthodox mission, but his monophysite consort Theodora had it intercepted with a mission of her own!

In the case of Palestine, and more remarkably in Syria, monophysite communities existed side by side with orthodox communities (in these cases as early as the fifth century). A monophysite bishop at Antioch! There were pitched battles in the streets.

It is at this point—as early as the fifth century—that one begins to wonder whether the "monophysites" are still theologically serious outside of Egypt. If the Eastern emperor happens to be monophysite, the East is monophysite. Then he is a Chalcedonian, and the East returns to orthodoxy. Now that its founder Eutyches is gone, is monophysite anti-Chalcedonianism still genuinely a religious creed, demanding of its faithful a conscientious religious assent, or has it become just a national or racial chauvinism?

Differences between monophysitism and orthodoxy there surely are. Speaking broadly, one can identify the former as the pious and zealous religion of the desert monks, and the latter as the cool, steady religion of the hierarchy. But are there still *credal* divergencies? One suspects and hopes that credal divergencies are lessening if whole Churches go so easily from orthodox to monophysite to orthodox as early as the fifth century.

What is happening to monophysitism?

Our suspicions are verified. As a dogma, monophysitism is losing her Christological list; she is regaining an orthodox equilibrium; she is straightening up gradually from heresy towards pure schism. She is no longer nearly so interested in denying the true manhood of Christ as she is in not being, for instance, culturally hellenistic like orthodoxy. And now as the sixth century opens, a great monophysite patriarch is destined unwittingly to confirm her in this direction.

Severus of Antioch

It was the farthest thing from his mind. *Severus of Antioch* (fl. 522-538) was an energetic leader as well as a genuine theologian. His intention was precisely to halt the drift of monophysitism towards Chalcedonian orthodoxy: He wanted to bring credal monophysitism back to life, back where it belonged, back to a meaningful denial of Christ's full humanity. He condemned Leo's *Tome to Flavian;* he condemned Chalcedon's "two natures." What he wanted was for monophysitism to regain her identity as a theology and a religion instead of persisting as a nationalistic or cultural chauvinism. But he deceived himself. He condemned Christ's full humanity only because he thought full humanity involved a human person in Christ (as indeed it does in us). He repudiated Eutyches, the very founder of monophysitism. *He condemned Chalcedon because to him Chalcedon was Nestorian.* He condemned Chalcedon because he did not make the distinction which is today so familiar to us, between person and nature. He was convinced that in giving Christ two natures Chalcedon had made him two beings.

In other words, Severus saw in the notion of two natures a rejection of Cyril's "One nature, incarnate, of the Word of God." He did not realize that in defining "two natures" Chalcedon had simply paraphrased Cyril: "One nature . . . of the Word of God" means divine nature; ". . . incarnate . . ." means human nature. Chalcedon had simply repeated clearly what Cyril had formulated ambiguously.

Let us not judge too harshly, however, either the monophysites of today or Severus of yesterday. After all, the notion of a single person in two distinct natures constitutes a strict mystery of faith, one whose depths we shall never fathom even in eternity. And so it came about that, at the dawn of the sixth century, Severus, patriarch of Antioch, the greatest monophysite theologian of all time, intending to divorce monophysitism once and for all from Chalcedonian orthodoxy, condemned Chalcedon, but condemned it only for a Nestorianism it had never proclaimed, and thus paradoxically aligned monophysitism with Chalcedonian orthodoxy.

The "Monophysitism" of our own time seems to be the "monophysitism" of Severus of Antioch: an orthodoxy that stresses the oneness of Christ's person by use of the term "nature," erroneously claiming thereby to reject Chalcedon. A happy error, if error there has to be.

The work of Severus, theologian and organizer, was crowned by Jacob Baradaeus, the fabled character who traveled the East from Asia to Egypt in disguise (to evade the orthodox emperor, Justinian), consecrating bishops and ordaining priests, restoring the see of Antioch to monophysitism (Severus' Antioch had of course gone orthodox at Justinian's accession)—in a word, restoring and solidifying the monophysite organization all over the East under the very nose of *the* Christian emperor par excellence. The tiny monophysite Church of Syria bears the well-deserved name of Jacobite to our very day.

The Indestructibility of "Nestorianism"

For eight hundred years the Nestorian Church was, with fluctuations of prosperity, a mighty organization, one whose missionary enterprise is unsurpassed in the history of Christianity. It had twenty-five metropolitan sees with probably two hundred bishoprics and as many monasteries, extending to China and India; but the time of its greatest expansion was soon followed by utter ruin. At the end of the fourteenth century the Mongol hordes of Timur Leng devastated Asia, sweeping away the Nestorian Church in a cataclysm of blood and apostasy . . .

In the succeeding five hundred years the remnants of the Nestorians were weakened by internal quarrels, leading to sub-schisms and to reunions with Rome. During the nineteenth century they were further reduced by the Kurdish massacres on the one hand and the activities of

American Protestant and Russian Orthodox missionaries on the other. During the war of 1914-1918 they again suffered massacre from the Turks and Kurds . . .[2] But today there are still about 200,000 Nestorians in the world, mostly in and near Iraq. They claim Nestorius for their doctor, but their credal allegiance is really to the less extreme doctrine of Nestorius' master, Theodore of Mopsuestia.[3]

We shall not attempt to retrace the "orthodoxization" of Nestorianism, even to the sketchy extent of our outline of the theological enterprise of Severus the monophysite. Suffice it to say that today's Nestorian schism, indeed the whole 1500-year Nestorian schism, is only very doubtfully heretical. Abandoning the radical, truly heretical theology of Nestorius, Nestorianism settled down very early to a one-sided orthodoxy stressing a legitimate point: the real distinction between Christ's godhead and manhood. Danger there is, as always, when a two-faceted mystery is so positioned that one facet is more in view than the other. But heresy there is not if the other facet (in this case the concrete unity of Christ's being, what we call his unity of person) is not denied.

The Fifth Ecumenical Council: Constantinople II (553)

Two centuries after Constantine, Justinian assumed an even more patronizing role. Less than some Caesar-popes of Czarist Russia, more than the secular arm of the medieval Latin Church, Constantine and Justinian were each successively looked upon as the Church's eldest son and protector, sent by God to protect her freedom and watch her theology.[4] The great Roman corpus of laws, the *Codex Justinianus,* opens

2 Donald Attwater, *The Eastern Churches* (London: Catholic Truth Society, n.d.), pp. 3-4.
3 Recall chapter 5.
4 But there was an important difference between Constantine and Justinian. Justinian crowned a tendency that had been developing ever since Constantine: Justinian was a real theologian.
    And there was a second important difference: Justinian's imperial consort was a monophysite. And Theodora wielded a genuine imperial authority comparable to that of her spouse, the orthodox emperor.

"In the name of Our Lord Jesus Christ," and continues with a definition of the Trinity and the Christian faith. Theological anathemata are to be found side by side with penalties laid down for criminal and civil transgressions. When Palestine erupted at the dawn of the sixth century in a monastic mystique of exaggerated deification, traceable back through the tenacious school of that great ascetic but poor theologian Evagrius of Pontus (fourth century) to Origen (third century), the emperor himself condemned ten "Origenist propositions," and then condemned Evagrius.

A certain insight into this paternalism on the part of the emperor towards the Church, and into the filial admiration and fear the Church had for her emperor, is indispensable if the reader is to comprehend what Hughes has called the "strangest of all the general councils."

Justinian proposed as his major imperial task the reunion of his monophysites with his own orthodoxy. The "monophysites," he reasoned (and we have seen), were now really much more anti-Nestorian than heretical, and condemned Chalcedon only for its seeming Nestorianism. Therefore Justinian need only seem to repudiate Chalcedon to the satisfaction of the monophysites, and the desired reunion would take place. It would of course be a most delicate operation, for Chalcedon had been an ecumenical council, an emperor's council accepted by the whole orthodox world. A Christian emperor could never reject a Christian emperor's council, nor would orthodoxy countenance the rejection if he did. Yet perhaps somehow the "monophysites" could be made to think that their beloved Cyril ("One nature, incarnate, of the Word of God"), whom they counted overthrown at Chalcedon, had been solemnly reinstated in a kind of overthrow of Chalcedon. The conditions required for the operation were clear, if delicate: It must seem to the monophysites to repudiate Chalcedon, and seem to the orthodox not to repudiate it. (Of course, if the operation were to backfire, so that, just in reverse, the *orthodox* saw a repudiation of their Chalcedon, and the *monophysites* saw no repudiation of Chalcedon . . . ! But let's not even think of that.)

Justinian's strategy was as canny as the undertaking would be delicate: He would condemn, without condemning Chalcedon, two strongly anti-monophysite Chalcedonian theologians, and for good measure would also condemn Nestorius' almost-heretical predecessor, Theodore of Mopsuestia. This ought to convince the monophysites that Ephesus' condemnation of Nestorius was still in effect in spite of the subsequent Chalcedon. It was risky business, since the two Chalcedonians in question had been explicitly approved by Chalcedon, and Justinian dared not risk an overt repudiation of the Council. But he would risk an implied repudiation of the Council in an overt repudiation of its theologians. The reunion of the monophysites was at stake.

Justinian went into action. He ordered "Three Chapters" (i.e., summaries) drawn up, one for each of the three theologians in question: Theodore and the two Chalcedonians, Theodoret of Cyr and Ibas of Edessa. Each "Chapter" *purported* to capsulize the "Nestorian errors" of one of the three. The Emperor then proposed these Three Chapters to the patriarchs for solemn condemnation.

The Eastern patriarchs signed, conditionally. Their condemnation would take effect the moment it was signed by the patriarch of the West. Justinian could rub his hands with glee—of course the pope would sign a document somewhat inimical to Chalcedon! The pope, Vigilius, was after all the creature of the monophysite empress, Theodora!

The pope may have been the creature of a monophysite Eastern empress, but he was patriarch of an unshakably Chalcedonian West. To condemn the Three Chapters, condemning three theologians who had lived and died a hundred years before in peace and communion with Holy Church, including two whose orthodoxy had been solemnly acclaimed by Chalcedon, would have been in the eyes of the West simply a prelude to a future repudiation of Chalcedon itself. The pope would not sign.

The pope was arrested—but he would not sign. He was abducted and still refused to sign. Despite his advanced age he was shipped to Constantinople, browbeaten for months—

but he remained unshaken. (In fact, he only took the opportunity of his sojourn to excommunicate the patriarch of Constantinople for having signed conditionally.) Two years' harassment at Constantinople did not break his will. Finally he hit
upon a rather canny plan of his own: He would write up his
own condemnation of the Three Chapters, and sign that.
Justinian acceded. Vigilius thereupon composed, and signed,
a condemnation of the Three Chapters—meticulously
emasculated.

But the predictable occurred instantly. The West deserted
the pope who had seemed to desert Chalcedon. The Western
bishops were far too busy protecting women and children and
churches from the barbarians to fathom the subtle differences
between Severian monophysitism and Chalcedon, or between
the condemnation the emperor wanted signed and the version
the pope had composed himself. The West knew one thing,
and knew it with the certitude of divine faith: Chalcedon had
been orthodox. And a pope had signed some document to
satisfy the anti-Chalcedonian monophysites.

The plan was backfiring. The monophysites were not back
in, and now the whole West was out. Pope and emperor then
agreed to call an ecumenical council. But when the emperor
unilaterally condemned the Three Chapters in its original form,
the form the pope had never signed, the pope threw up the
council project and took flight. The imperial troops trapped
him in a church. They crashed the doors, cornered Vigilius
in the sanctuary, and manhandled the octogenarian so bar-
barously that they themselves now had to flee for their lives
from the mob that had crowded into the church behind them.

The pope was again in custody. But he refused to attend the
emperor's Ecumenical Council V. He did agree to work
privately, again, on his *own* condemnation of the Three
Chapters while the emperor was busy guiding the council
through theirs.

And so while the fathers of the fifth ecumenical council,
Constantinople II, under the personal presidency of Emperor
Justinian, vied with one another to see which could condemn
the Three Chapters the longest and the loudest, Vigilius was

privately composing his own condemnation of the Three Chapters. The reader has already guessed. Vigilius emasculated them again.

So Justinian pressured Vigilius for still another year. The decade of harassment at last took its toll. The ancient Vigilius solemnly approved the fifth ecumenical council and all its condemnations, condemned the Three Chapters, and died.

Vigilius' companion and sole moral support to the bitter end, a deacon named Pelagius, was elected his successor. This Pope Pelagius at once undertook to explain to his Western patriarchate that Constantinople II *had condemned nothing of Chalcedon except the possibility of Nestorian misinterpretation.* His persuading was in vain. It was more than a hundred years before the West completely restored union with the see of Rome.

Long, confused, violent, childish, cruel, pitiful story. We are embarrassed at having taken the reader so far afield from his pure intellectual pursuit of currents of thought. But how else could we have showed him better that there are no currents of thought, that there are only currents of thinkers, and that when the thinkers are little, and striving for political goals, the thinking is shallow. But if it is Christian orthodoxy that is at stake, the Spirit of truth will undertake the most unlikely and astonishing means of preserving it. Pope Pelagius is right: The fifth ecumenical council condemned Nestorianism; it did not condemn the fourth ecumenical council. The ratification of the dying Vigilius cannot be interpreted in any other sense.

Egregius Doctor: Gregory the Great

Ranked with Augustine, Jerome, and Ambrose as one of the very greatest fathers of the Western Church, *Gregory* (fl. 590-604) probably deserves it the least. But he surely deserves it more than has often been thought.

Gregory has always been recognized as a historic figure.

He was the first monk to occupy the chair of Peter. He wielded remarkable influence on the spirituality of the diocesan clergy: His *Pastoral Care* became for the secular priest of the Middle Ages what Benedict's *Rule* was for the monk. His reign constitutes a landmark in the history of the constantly centralizing ecclesiastical administration of the West: He extended his direct supervision to include the dioceses of peninsular Italy after the manner of Alexandria's mastery of the bishops of Egypt. He was master even of the West's other metropolitan sees—to the extent he could maintain his overextended lines of communication. He is a great historical figure, and this has never been denied.

But as an exegete, a preacher and a hagiographer, does Gregory deserve his traditional rank among the four Latin "great doctors"? What does it matter, asks Gregory, who wrote the book of Job? Why, in any case it was the Holy Spirit! The scholarly embarrassment of the scientific West at an "exegete" who could write a line like that, an exegete who wrote his exegeses without so much as bothering to read any other commentaries, has only recently been replaced with admiration for a man who could write a line like that. After all, whoever wrote Job or any other biblical book—indeed whether Job belongs to the genre of history in the modern sense of the word or to some other genre—what is most important, modern biblical theologians tell us, is what the divine author of Job is teaching us in the book, of which he himself composed every verse, that it is God alone who is master of good and evil. Our biblical theologians of course improve immensely upon Gregory in their esteem for solid "lower criticism." They are also concerned to identify the authors actually responsible for each book of the bible. It is important to know at least the general identity of the human author, with his personal mentality, literary style and genre, and racial or national culture, so as to know what the divine author meant when, together, *they* wrote the book.

Gregory probably does, then, deserve to rank with the four, even if only as number four.

The Death of Western Patristic Theology

The barbarian invasions have now killed genuine theology in the West. Western civilization is fighting for its existence, not for its currents of thought.[5] The West will have to await the dawn of scholasticism for its theological rebirth. And that will be a wait of five or six centuries, as long a night as the West's great patristic day. But what a rebirth! Grand enough to compensate in large measure for such a long theological sleep. (Grand enough to tempt the West to neglect the fathers one day, especially the Eastern fathers, in favor of a late scholasticism far inferior to the great scholastic dawn.) But at the beginning of the seventh century we bid the West: Good night, sleep well! You cannot die. The body of Christ is immortal. We attend your waking.

The Sixth Ecumenical Council: Constantinople III (680-681)

The fifth ecumenical council had been no dearer to the hearts of the monophysites than to the Latins. The Latins at length understood and returned from schism, but the monophysites remained obstinate. Was it because there was so little heresy to return from? Was it schism for the sake of schism? The obstacle was perhaps only the determination of Egypt and Syria to remain culturally schismatic from hellenism.

But heretical or not, monophysitism continued to be considered heresy by the orthodox. And a whole century after the fifth ecumenical council, orthodoxy was still as willing as Justinian to go to any lengths to win her back. This time instead of an emperor it was a patriarch of Constantinople. To convince the monophysites that orthodoxy considered Christ to

---

5 Western piety and a rich religious culture never died. Witness the elaboration of the splendors of the Roman liturgy precisely during the "Dark Ages." The West preserved her faith, and thereby all the essentials of her theology elaborated in centuries past. But original theological thinking was gone. (From 636 on? The "last Western father," Isidore of Seville, died in that year.)

be one single divine being, and not two complete beings, one divine and one human, Constantinople's patriarch, Sergius, declared that *all Christ's activities and choices are divine.* Christ performs no human activities, his true manhood notwithstanding.

Unlike the intricate machinations of Justinian, this simple move succeeded. There was nothing complex about it at all. At long last the monophysites saw that the orthodox could not be Nestorians in disguise. An act of union was signed. Christianity was no longer divided.

Unfortunately, Sergius' doctrine was false. It was simple monophysitism. What the patriarch was trying to prove was true enough: that orthodoxy, in attributing to Christ two complete natures, did not attribute to him two complete beings. In the concrete, he is only a divine being—a divine Person. But the way the patriarch undertook to explain this truth—depriving Christ's human nature of all human activity and human choice —amounted to depriving him of his human nature. The monophysites crowded delightedly back into the fold.

True it is that since Christ's only Person is divine, all his activities and choices are therefore the activity and choices *of God personally,* from being born to walking along a road to dying on the cross to rising from the dead. God was born, God walked, God died, God rose. This is Christian truth. But it is not true to say that all these activities and choices are *divine activities and choices;* it is not true to say, as the patriarch of Constantinople was implying, that all these activities, some of them seemingly human, really proceeded through the divine nature of Christ, so that his human nature was bereft of all activity and choice. After all, some of Christ's activities, if Christ is to have a real human nature, proceed through his human nature and will (like his prayer and decision in Gethsemane, "Not my will but thine be done")—while others indeed proceed through his divine nature and will (like rising from the dead).

In a word, *some of the activities and choices of God are not divine but human* in God-become-man. The patriarch had erred.[6] The error was to be condemned in the sixth ecumenical council.

But before any suggestion of convoking an ecumenical council to pass judgment upon so simple and clear a proposition, Rome was simply asked for her theological opinion. Would that she had rejected Constantinople's surreptitious monophysite doctrine that all Christ's activities and choices, human though they might have seemed to the casual onlooker, were really divine. But no, Rome was asked for her opinion in a rather routine way, and Pope Honorius granted a rather routine approval, stating casually that *there could never be any conflict* between the activities of Christ's two natures.

Honorius had of course missed the point. Monothelitism (Greek term for "one-will-ism") does not stop at the Christian doctrine that Christ as man always acted *in accordance with* his nature as God, that Christ's human will never contradicted his divine will. Monothelitism goes further, and states heretically that Christ *never acted as man* at all, never made human choices. The pope had not answered the question.

But if Rome had missed Constantinople's point, Jerusalem had not. Jerusalem's new patriarch caught the pope up short in a rather strong letter, reminding him that Christ had two wills, human and divine. Whereupon Pope Honorius missed the point again. Somewhat exasperated, we may well imagine, he saw fit to remind Jerusalem that Christ had only *one will*. How could his human will contradict his divine will?

Obviously, by "one will in Christ" Honorius means once again "agreement of two wills," the human being always subject to the divine. Honorius could not be brought to realize that *he was being asked whether or not Christ had two will-faculties,* not whether they always acted in unison.

Honorius had now twice misunderstood the question and answered both times that Constantinople was orthodox in pro-

---

[6] The heresy is to be called monergism, or monothelitism, depending upon whether one refers to Christ's activities in general or to his will-acts in particular. They both come to the same thing practically, since will-acts are activities of a person through a nature. Hence the form "monothelitism" is usually employed to cover the heretical doctrine that all Christ's activities, all his will-acts included, are divine.

claiming but one will in Christ. Actually Constantinople's proposition was clear monophysitism. In denying an *active* human nature in Christ, Constantinople was implicitly denying a genuine human nature.

The pope had *meant* a harmony of two wills. But he had *said*—word for word—"one will."

The East took him literally. One will in Christ, the divine will of his Godhead, with no will in his manhood. And the emperor made it law.

Five years later another pope clarified Honorius, stating very clearly that while there could be no conflict between Christ's two wills, he nonetheless had two distinct wills, one in each of his natures. But it was too late. The return of the "monophysites" to "orthodoxy" was too precious for the emperor to brook any papal interference at this late date. The emperor quickly reaffirmed monothelitism as the law of the land in an edict forbidding further discussion.

Too late? We have not reckoned with Martin I, the pope elected just after this latest imperial edict. In the great Lateran Synod of 649 Martin condemned monothelitism and promulgated the condemnation all over the world.

Martin's insubordination of course provoked prompt imperial reaction. The emperor was not kind. Dragging Martin through the streets of Constantinople in rags and chains, he deigned to commute the death sentence only at the merciful behest of the patriarch of Constantinople, who felt Constantinople already guilty enough in initiating and continuing the whole affair. But the commutation was an exile so cruel that Martin died within a few months.

A generation later Martin's stand at the Lateran Synod was vindicated. A later pope and a later emperor convoked the sixth ecumenical council (Constantinople III). After a thorough debate lasting a year, an overwhelming majority voted to insist upon the two wills and two activities of Christ. As usual, the emperor confirmed the council by law. Orthodoxy had won at last.

Maximus the Confessor

The real hero of the sixth ecumenical council never lived to see it.

Pope Martin's Lateran Synod had broken the back of monothelitism a generation before the ecumenical council by showing it in its true colors as monophysitism in disguise. The council merely affirmed the decision of the much earlier Lateran Synod.

The theologian of the Lateran Synod had been *Maximus the Confessor* (fl. ca. 620-662). For decades an inveterate anti-monophysite, he seems, nonetheless, to have been almost as slow as the rest of the East to recognize monothelitism as surreptitious monophysitism. But as an old man he moved against the new brand of monophysitism with the vigor he had shown in his younger days against monophysitism pure and simple, and he conquered. Nearly seventy, he secured a condemnation of monothelitism at Martin's Lateran Synod—for which affront to a monothelite emperor he eventually paid with his tongue and right hand, in that classic barbarity of condign justice by which a speaker and writer forfeited the conjoined instruments of his felony. The mutilations were too cruel for the aged man; Maximus died in the very year of his glorious "confession."

But Maximus is more than a conquering orthodox polemicist and confessor to the death. He is the positive theoretician of an ascetical and mystical theology which marks him as the last of the great original thinkers of the patristic Church— the only father of the Church between Gregory the Great and John of Damascus.

Maximus had long been thought of as a mere compiler in the spirit of the late Greek eclectics, without much originality and without internal consistency. But toward the middle of the twentieth century, scholars began to recognize in Maximus an eclectic of towering synthetic originality, in whom hard-to-manage sources like Origen, Evagrius and "Denis the Areopagite" find not only reconciliation and synthesis, but genuine orthodoxy. This is a feat unparalleled in the history of the ancient Church. The result is a consistent, profound, and thoroughly Christian view of our coming forth from God, our fall, and our return to the life of God in a participated deification of the whole cosmos.

The End of the Patristic Era

It would be high-handed as well as hasty to condemn as decadent the centuries that saw the *rise* of the compilers, the fifth century (e.g., Cyril of Alexandria) to the seventh (e.g., Maximus the Confessor). After all, it was scarcely the task of the fathers to initiate currents of thought in an age when the theological quarrels, whether Christological or mystical, already had their theoretical solutions in currents initiated before. From the fifth to the seventh centuries the task of patristic theology was precisely compilation. The theology needed to defeat the current heresies had already been evolved. It remained only to be applied where and when needed. Hence the legitimacy of the new genre of compilations and "chains" of quotations from earlier writers.

True, a compiler erred when he truncated a text—cut it off in mid-paragraph because the dogmatic "point" had been made—regardless of whether or not the point had been seen in the dogmatic context of which it formed a part. We commit the same error today when we utilize the fathers as a thesaurus of short citations instead of involving whole contexts which bear upon the thesis which we wish to prove. A compiler erred, then, when he truncated texts; and he erred again when his chain of citations from earlier fathers linked texts which in context do not link. But he scarcely erred simply because he compiled. The task of the fifth, sixth, and seventh centuries was precisely to compile the old arguments, already theologically complete but scattered hither and yon, against old heresies that dragged on and on. The Church's need for original thinkers had been replaced by a need for dogged thinkers. These were the compilers.

Nor must we forget the exceptional authors of the compiler centuries, who were not mere compilers, like Gregory the Great, Isidore of Seville, or the brilliant and original Maximus the Confessor. Nor again the fine precisions of the monothelite controversy and the sixth ecumenical council.

Therefore the later and less important centuries of the patristic Church, the fifth, sixth, and seventh centuries, though dominated by compilers, do not represent pure decadence. But they herald it. There will come a time when the ancient, classical heresies no longer present a real danger: the eighth century. And the compilers will continue merely compiling from the works that defeated the heresies. One could wish they had profited by the theological peace to water the immensely fertile soil of the dogmatic development of earlier centuries. One could wish they had undertaken a deeper and fuller elaboration of the theology of the Holy Spirit (which incidentally might have forestalled some of today's misunderstanding between East and West concerning the procession of the Holy Spirit). One could wish they had harvested the doctrine of man's divinization, planted in the New Testament, watered by Justin, Irenaeus, Clement of Alexandria, Hippolytus, and Methodius, systematically cultivated by Athanasius, Gregory of Nyssa, Cyril, "Denis," and finally by Maximus the Confessor.[7] (Such a harvest could have forestalled much of what was sterile in the scholastic controversies on grace and free will.) But no, instead of exploiting the theological peace to bring to perfection doctrines well begun but not fully elaborated, the eighth-century compilers simply continued what their predecessors had done during the three preceeding centuries of genuine need: They kept compiling.

Ideally, or idealistically, after the demise of the great heretical threats, the fifth, sixth, and seventh century compilers should have given place in the eighth century to a new sort of father, who would build upon the incredibly rich patrimony of

[7] If it is true that the twelfth-century Western rebirth of a theology of grace, rich and promising, emerged later in an elaboration of a doctrine of sanctifying grace "instead of, and in place of, a theology of divinization," as Dalmais asserts ("Patristique grecque," article "Divinisation," *Dictionnaire de la spiritualité,* volume 3, column 1389), then, while very grateful for a theology of created grace, one asks oneself whether perhaps the Eastern doctrine of man's deification is not the greatest single loss suffered by the West as a result of the schism.

his forebears—the trinitarian theology, the Christology, and the mystical theology of the great men who had gone before. (This is a dream ironically idealistic in ourselves, who have scarcely begun the same task in the twentieth century.) But no, the eighth century writers continued what their predecessors had so aptly begun. They compiled.

Then let patristic theology be at rest. Let us have some one truly great compiler, and then let the patristic centuries come to an end. It is *John of Damascus* (fl. 726-730), last of the fathers of the Church, who in his *The Orthodox Faith* so admirably summarizes (if with uneven judiciousness) the orthodox Christian faith, established by Jesus Christ, presented in sacred scripture, and so richly elaborated and jealously preserved by the "fathers of the Church" through seven hundred years from Clement of Rome to Damascene himself.

That patristic elaboration we now invite the reader to examine in depth and detail in the very writings of the fathers of the Church. We promise him hours of fascination and satisfaction.

QUESTIONS FOR DISCUSSION

1. Why did Egypt go monophysite? (Give two reasons.)
2. What weakened early Egyptian monophysitism? Give an example.
3. Recount the evangelization of Ethiopia.
4. Who is later monophysitism's great theologian? What were his theological intentions? What were the unintended results, and why? In other words, why is it uncertain that monophysitism is still a heresy and not just a schism?
5. Identify Jacob Baradaeus.
6. Why is it uncertain that Nestorianism is heretical today?
7. Describe briefly Emperor Justinian's Code of Laws as an example of his influence in the Church.
8. Describe Justinian's delicate plan for the recall of the monophysites to Christian unity.

9. Describe the place of the Three Chapters in Justinian's plan for the return of the monophysites.
10. Which patriarchs condemned the Three Chapters, and subject to what condition?
11. Describe Justinian's efforts to obtain a final condemnation of the Three Chapters by the patriarch of the West.
12. Why was the pope afraid to condemn the Three Chapters? Were his fears justifiable?
13. Justinian's plan worked just in reverse. Recount the story.
14. How did Pope Vigilius twice thwart Justinian?
15. At last Vigilius gave in and condemned the Three Chapters as Justinian wanted them condemned. Is this not a pope's condemnation of an ecumenical council (Chalcedon)?
16. Why have modern theologians been a little embarrassed about Pope Gregory the Great? Why are they less embarrassed today?
17. What caused the death of Western theology? How long had it lived? How long did it have to await a rebirth, and what form did this rebirth take?
18. What new doctrine did Sergius, Patriarch of Constantinople, propose as bait for the monophysites? Why is the doctrine false? Be sure you can give history's traditional name for it.
19. Why did Rome fail to fight the error?
20. Several years after Rome's failure to condemn the error, she reversed herself. What was the name and fate of the pope who achieved this? What was the emperor's motivation for protecting the false teaching?
21. The Roman condemnation referred to in question 20 is mostly the polemical achievement of one theologian. What is his name and where did he achieve his triumph during his lifetime? What was his reward? But he was more than a polemicist. What is his even greater contribution to theology? Why have you never heard of him?
22. What was the task of the fathers of the fifth, sixth, and seventh centuries, and how did they fulfill it?

23. Why did patristic theology die (in the eighth century)? What did it leave undone for us to do today?
24. Who is the last father of the Church, and what manner of writing did he do? What is the name of his best-known work?

FURTHER PROBLEMS

1. What likelihood is there that distressing episodes like those recounted in chapter 6 might be repeated in the foreseeable future? Discuss your reasons.
2. We repeat the discussion problem proposed before chapter 1: How would you organize patristic studies as part of the framework of twentieth-century theology? In other words, what should be the function of patrology in the twentieth-century effort to preserve and elaborate Christian truth?

INDEX

120